THE SKATE-BOARD BOOK

Revised Edition

THE SKATE-BOARD BOOK

BEN DAVIDSON Revised Edition

GROSSET & DUNLAP
Publishers   New York
A Filmways Company

Library of Congress Catalog card number: 76-8036
ISBN 0-448-12484-X
ISBN 0-448-13383-0 (Library Edition)

First printing revised edition 1979

Printed in the United States of America

Credits

Photography: Ben Davidson, Ray Johnson

Drawings: Julie Svendsen

Acknowledgments

My sincere thanks to the following for their help in putting this book together: Mark Richards (Val Surf, North Hollywood, California), Tom Sims (Sims Skateboards, Whittier, California), Jack Dimon (Pro/Am Skateboard Racers Association), Warren Bolster (*Skateboarder* magazine), Dave Abell, Roger, Chris, and Doug.

CON-TENTS

Foreword 11

1. The Roots 13
2. What to Buy and Why 22
   Boards
   Trucks
   Wheels
3. Safety: Practices and Equipment 44
   "Tune Your Board"
   Equipment
   Safety Begins Within
   Falling
4. The Art 53
5. Freestyle Tricks 64
   Body-Position Tricks
   Balance
   Board Control
   Body Control
   Strength
6. Repair and Maintenance 83
7. Competition Skating 94
8. Skateboard Organizations 103
9. Skateparks: From Drainage Basins to Cement Waves 106
   Index 117

THE SKATE-BOARD BOOK

FORE-WORD

What a contradiction!

On the one hand there's skateboarding, just like any other sport in its potential for enjoyment, challenge, beauty, and benefit to the body. Then on the other hand there's skateboarding, the most frequent cause of childhood accidents—outlawed in numerous American cities from Rhode Island to California and considered by many to be a menace to pedestrians as well as drivers.

The key to the irony is the word "sport." Obviously some don't see skateboarding as a sport at all. Some may believe that, even though a sport by most standards, its athletic potential is abused. No doubt those who swell the serious-accident records have ignored or overlooked the physical and mental responsibilities that go along with any sport.

It's truly a two-sided issue, but maybe not for long. In terms of established athletics, skateboarding is very new. And in all probability, its present status is somewhere between the simple street fun it once was and the highly developed sport it is already becoming.

The fact is, however, that like skiing, automobile racing, and other high-speed sports, without understanding, proper equipment, and a step-by-step approach to mastery, skateboarding is blatantly unsafe. Cuts, bruises, broken teeth, and concussions from skateboard accidents unfortunately aren't a rarity, and unless you're just going to cruise slowly up and down your block in straight lines, a casual attitude toward the sport is self-destructive. Ultimately it becomes a matter of concrete, flesh, and bones.

The first step, then, in reaping the benefits of skateboarding is knowledge. Without it, the chances of your posing a threat to yourself and the public are vastly increased. In the end, all concerned suffer—either by involvement in accidents or through creation of negative public opinion.

Enjoyment and low-risk challenge, this is what skateboarding holds for the knowledgeable, practical rider. And that, in a nutshell, is the reason for this book. Perhaps it's too obvious to even mention, but I've seen too many carved-up faces and twisted bodies to let it go unsaid. And besides, it wouldn't be a bad idea to keep the irony clear in your mind, especially after you've finished the book and become involved in the sport.

THE 1 ROOTS

About 5,000 years ago human beings hit on the idea of the wheel. Since that time our fascination with this basic mechanical object has flowered. In fact, it's almost impossible to conceive of a world devoid of wheels. In one sense, it might be a simpler world, but it would surely be a less interesting and more back-breaking one. That pretty well sums it up, but it's really an oversimplified view. For, although we take it for granted, the wheel to a large extent has helped form not only our pattern of activity, but our thinking as well.

I don't know exactly how long it took man to realize that the wheel could provide hundreds of forms of recreation as well. But I'd bet it wasn't long before our ancestors were rolling things back and forth to each other and racing ox carts around the fields (oxen aren't too fast but anything beats moping around a hut in your free time).

So, century upon century passes, and one day someone hacks apart a pair of roller skates and nails them to a two-by-four. Voilà, a new toy.

It's really impossible to pinpoint "the beginning of skateboarding." Some say it began happening in the early sixties, some say in the fifties, and a few

people whom I've talked to say they were into a crude form of the sport while they were growing up in the thirties and forties. That's not hard to understand considering that, at its simplest, the skateboard is pretty uncomplicated.

One thing is for sure: around 1962, skateboarding suddenly broke out of the realm of casual play and began to take on the characteristics not only of a fad but of a sport. Until that time, it was a matter of building your own, probably breaking it, and then losing interest immediately. But when southern California surfers began to realize the potential of skateboarding as a substitute (not necessarily a good one) for their first love, the sport took off.

There's a lot of concrete in this world and, unlike waves, it's always there. It's hard and it doesn't move beneath you, but you can move above it. Sidewalk surfing was a logical step, and soon it began to catch on. For some, it became almost addictive.

In that first year, 1962, when it was starting to look like the whole thing might have possibilities, the people from Val Surf, a surf shop in North Hollywood, California, approached the Chicago Roller Skate Company with an idea. The way they saw it, there was no point in chopping up used roller skates and nailing them to misshapen, poor-quality boards. If Chicago would sell them the already separated trucks (the assembly that holds the axle and cushions the ride) and wheels, they could begin to develop production of skateboards in a standardized, systematic way.

According to Mark Richards, who now manages Val Surf, Chicago wasn't too hot on the idea. For whatever reason, they just weren't ready to disfigure one of the finest roller skates on the market. Eventually that year, however, they came around, and Val Surf found itself in a new world—the skateboard market. With high school students shaping the boards and mounting the truck assemblies, Val Surf began cranking out skateboards, selling them as fast as they could make them.

Within the next three years, skateboarding spread east like a brushfire. Jan and Dean started singing about it, the news media began reporting about it, and skateboard manufacturers began making a bundle off of it. By 1965 the country was fully tuned in to the new fad. Competitions were being sponsored by local parks and recreation departments, and skateboarders were finding that what once seemed like a toy was becoming a source of athletic pride.

But it wasn't all roses by any means. In fact, during 1965 the game began to sour in a bad way. As fast as it picked up adherents that's how fast skateboarding attracted criticism, often to the point of outrage. The underlying reason was clear: to many people, it was a nuisance. The harsh sound of hard wheels clattering on concrete and the fear (and actual instances) of running over or being run over by skateboarders were a plain and simple drag to those who had no athletic or financial interest in the sport.

And then came the clincher. The California Medical Association announced that skateboarding accidents were rapidly overtaking bicycle accidents as the major cause of childhood injuries. The fact that nearly one third of all skateboarding injuries were received by adults didn't lessen the impact of the CMA's report. A new log had been thrown on the fire of opposition that was closing in on skateboarding.

Cities from San Diego, California, to Providence, Rhode Island, enacted ordinances banning skateboarding on public streets. Other cities began to apply existing traffic laws to skateboarders in an effort to reduce "the menace." Some cities tried and failed, but the spirit was there. Suddenly the general public lost its curiosity and began coming down hard on skateboarding. And then, just as suddenly, the sport virtually vanished. Warehouses were full of worthless skateboards and skateboard parts. Several manufacturers were burned in a big way. *Skateboarder* magazine, which had put out four issues, ceased publication. In every sense, the party was over.

But the bad publicity, the public outcry, and the legal actions don't tell the whole story. They don't really explain how such a hot idea could be here one day and gone the next. A lot of people say, "Well, it's that way with any fad, they just come and go." To a certain extent that's not too far from the truth. People do latch on to a seemingly exciting thing, but it's not until they've fully used it, taken it to its limits, and then lost interest in it that the activity or object disappears.

Skateboarding fit into this pattern perfectly. Although new materials such as fiberglass and aluminum were being incorporated into skateboards

even in 1965, innovations weren't widespread and basic deficiencies weren't being ironed out. For starters, there were the trucks. They had been designed basically for roller skates and utilized only one solid cushioning bushing. This severely impaired mobility. More critical, however, were the wheels. Again, borrowing from roller skate principles, skateboard manufacturers used only clay composition wheels. Hard and smooth, they provided roller skaters with a fast ride at relatively inexpensive prices. But the same quality that was a blessing for roller skaters was a disaster for skateboarders. Very simply, the composition wheels had awful traction. On roller skates, the problem was nonexistent because traction was gained through the use of both feet. With the wheels mounted on a single surface, though, the situation was totally different. Maneuvers which were more complicated than a slow turn could easily result in uncontrollable slide-outs. On top of

that, the hard wheels were treacherous on anything other than a smooth, clean surface. And, as if all that weren't enough, they were noisy—very noisy.

In short, the components from which skateboards were constructed weren't designed specifically for them and unfortunately didn't meet the basic requirements the sport demanded. In many ways, the mid-sixties skateboard was a toy. At best, it was doomed to extinction by its inadequacies. Skaters took their boards as far as they would go and when that limit was reached, there just wasn't any place left to go. Not that skaters didn't have a fairly good idea of what could theoretically be done or the ability to go that length; it was more like trying to break the land speed record in a Volkswagen.

But the gears of progress were turning even as skateboarding was in the deepest stage of its decade-long sleep. During the late sixties, urethane—a soft, durable plastic—was being molded into roller skate wheels. In limited quantity, they were introduced into roller skating rinks; the response to them, however, was strictly negative. The urethane innovation totally reversed the properties of skate wheels. Because they were softer, they were quieter and gripped better, but they were also slower. The reduction in

speed was a turnoff to roller skaters, who couldn't have cared less about increased traction. (As mentioned, traction on composition wheels is no problem when they're mounted on two skates.) Noise wasn't a problem for roller skaters either. Safe inside the roller rink, they were free of hassles from irate citizens.

The urethane roller skate wheel was a gigantic flop and remained so until 1973, when something happened that is usually considered the greatest advancement to date in skateboard construction. That year, Frank Nasworthy, a surfer from Encinitas, California, began toying with the idea of utilizing urethane wheels on a skateboard. Every quality of the material was suited to the purpose. The idea was brilliant. In conjunction with Creative Urethanes, Inc., a company that had been involved in urethane roller skate wheels, Cadillac Wheels introduced the first urethane wheel designed specifically for skateboarding. Slightly softer than the urethane roller skate wheel, the new wheel opened up possibilities that earlier skateboards could not offer.

Bang! Skateboarding began to take off again. Now fiberglass lamination became the thing in board fabrication. Although the process had been around for a long time and had been utilized in skateboards by Hobie in 1965, it took one Bob Bahne, a surfboard manufacturer also from Encinitas, to really see the potential of fiberglass boards. Using his knowledge of snow-ski dynamics, Bahne set out to produce a flexible board that would respond accurately to the rider and stand up to the passage of time. Together with his buddy Frank Nasworthy, Bahne quickly helped sweep the dust off skateboarding and bring it to the level of an art.

Now, here we are in the middle of it. Should we still look at it as a fad? Well, in certain respects it is. Skateboarding has suddenly exploded into popularity as all fads do. But fads also peter out and disappear. There's no question that there had already been a skateboard fad and that it had faded. Only time will tell what will happen with its current popularity. My own feeling is that the sport has been elevated to a point where it can't fall very far again. Perpetual innovation, competition, formal organization of skateboarders, and dedication by top skaters to the cause of establishing skateboarding as a recognized sport convince me that a new challenge has been born, a challenge that will continue as long as athletic skill remains a prized goal.

In many respects skateboarding has already become an established part of our society. Classes in skateboarding, skateboard parks, competition— all reveal an acceptance of the sport. If these things don't convince you that skateboarding is becoming a part of our daily lives, check this out: in November 1975, Emery Air Freight announced that some of their deliverymen were making their way through crowded city streets on, you guessed it, skateboards. A little more sinister was a story that appeared in the *Los Angeles Times* on August 3, 1975. It seems that two young men had walked into a doughnut shop on a major street in Sepulveda, California, held up the waitress, and stolen $125. Guess what they made their escape on?

Skateboarding is also becoming a lot safer, even though the degree of challenge is broadening. Wider, softer wheels are providing better traction. New alloys are replacing the brittle "pot metal" that was once used in trucks. And boards are generally sturdier and more stable. In addition, skateboard organizations are placing an increasingly strong emphasis on safety practices and equipment. Manufacturers are responding with plans for helmets, impact jackets, and pads specifically designed for skating. More is being written about the sport, and proper techniques of mastery are being developed and communicated.

Of course, problems still exist. Accidents are frequent, often resulting in serious injury and occasionally death. Inconsiderate skaters still threaten pedestrians (as well as themselves) and interfere with automobile traffic. And cities are still enforcing regulations on skateboarding. Traffic citations, fines, and safety lectures await skaters who are either ignorant of the law and commonsense practices or disregard them. But these problems can and must be eliminated, if skateboarding is to achieve the status it deserves.

We owe the sport that much because, if you know what you're doing, it's worth it. We always seem to look beyond the joy of an activity for some greater benefit, and the pleasure to be derived from skateboarding is enough of an incentive to get into it. But there is additional value: while you're having fun, you're also doing your body good. Not only does skateboarding afford basic exercise—because it's a speed sport that incorporates elements of balance and grace—but it can also help you confront and accept your physical limitations. This is a highly underrated aspect of many sports, but it can be crucial to personal development. In addition, the confidence you attain in mastering the various skating skills can give you a foundation for

self-confidence in other areas. And it's a challenge. Who can explain the importance of that? Suffice it to say that challenge is the stuff life's made of.

All this may sound a little heady. Coupled with the fact that speeds of fifty to sixty miles an hour have been attained and that there are skateboards on the market that retail for $75, it begins to look mighty impressive. But the fact of the matter is simply that skateboarding is a lot of fun. The beauty of it is that while skiing and surfing—the sports most akin to skateboarding —are restricted to certain climates and geographical areas, skateboarding can happen wherever there's concrete. And you don't have to look too far for that.

WHAT 2 TO BUY AND WHY

OUTSIDE OF SKILL, desire, and safety awareness, the most important thing in mastering skateboarding is a reliable piece of equipment, one suited to the type of skating you want to do. As with any sport, low-grade equipment that's incompatible with your needs detracts from the pleasure and can be downright dangerous. As skateboarding grows in popularity and intricacy, the volume of boards, trucks, wheels, and other component parts multiplies in a way that would make any businessman drool. The variety is ever increasing and, while most needs can readily be met with products now on the market, improvements will eventually accommodate even the most extreme skating variations.

Such quantity is, of course, a great benefit to skateboarders, but it can also be mind boggling. Where there's no selection, there's no decision. You just buy whatever's available. But where a hundred factors come into play, you take on the role of the demanding consumer—shopping around, experimenting, and gathering all the information you can get your hands on. Selecting a skateboard is almost as much a skill as riding one.

Not only should you know what's available and what you need but, as the saying goes, "buyer beware." You have to expect it. Some skateboard equipment is junk, and many manufacturers and retailers will lay that junk on you with one hand and snatch up your money with the other. The best way to combat the inevitable scoundrel is to have some idea of what to look for; ask questions and try out components before you buy them. Don't be sold. Most salesmen will respond to your inquiries readily, and those who don't will probably come around when they see you mean business.

As for the best place to go for skateboard equipment, a lot of skateboard shops are popping up and many surf shops carry an extensive product line. You'll find the most knowledgeable salesmen in these types of stores, many of them into skateboarding themselves. A sporting goods store is probably the next best source and after that a department store with a good overall selection of sports equipment and salesmen who work strictly in that area. The most unreliable source is the discount department store. Here, in general, you're going to find the lowest quality merchandise and salesmen who will almost certainly know less than you. Skateboards are usually sold preassembled in this type of store, with little or no variation in components. The materials and fabrication processes that go into this kind of board are low cost and low quality. Even a lack of funds shouldn't force you into a buying situation like this. In the long run you're going to lose out because the board you buy will most likely deteriorate in a number of ways and limit your freedom to advance your skill. It's better to hold off awhile, save your money, and invest in a board that won't let you down.

Buying directly from the manufacturer may save you some money and give you access to products that might not be available in your area. The key here is to know exactly what you're getting before you put any money in the mail. Research the product you're interested in. Send to the manufacturer for information and specifications and, if at all possible, find someone who owns or has owned the model you're considering buying. Try it out and ask for his or her opinion of it.

The most important thing is not to settle for something less than what you want. You can find just about anything if you know what you're after. Specific information on where to buy can be found through skateboard organizations, clubs, and publications.

With that in mind, let's take a look at skateboard components and some of the considerations involved in choosing the most efficient ones.

Boards

Boards can be classified in three basic ways, all essential to performance and reliability. The broadest category is degree of flexibility. In its earliest form, the skateboard was constructed of a solid, unlaminated wood board about one-half to three-quarters of an inch thick. The result was a stiff, unyielding board, usually very sturdy but limited by its rigidity. For a fast downhill run and certain handstand and jumping tricks, nothing beats a stiff board.

Many skaters still prefer stiff boards and use them exclusively, often with a high degree of success. But for the average rider, a rigid board is restricting. Although urethane wheels and improved truck assemblies have partially reversed some of the negative qualities of stiff boards, a more cushioned ride can be found. Enter the flex board.

The flex board has at least three advantages. First, flexibility allows the skater to easily employ "weighting and unweighting." This is a technique in which you push down on the board and then rise, keeping both feet on the board. Coupled with the proper torso movement, this helps build up and reduce speed regardless of incline and without pushing off. It's essential in slalom-type runs (where the pumping action enables you to accelerate around the gates), in maintaining speed on level ground, and in more accurately controlling speed on downhill runs.

Another advantage of flex boards is shock absorption. It's easy to see how a board that flexes up and down will cushion the ride over rough terrain. You can think of it as the difference between walking stiff-legged, pounding the ground with every step, and keeping your legs loose enough to walk over bumps and into holes without rattling your brains. As I said, improved wheels and trucks have taken some of the thump out of riding a stiff board, but flex is a lot easier to handle for the average rider.

Also, as you push down on a flex board, you lower your center of gravity, thus further enabling you to execute sharper turns. A low center of gravity allows race-car drivers to corner quickly and accurately. As leaning is the only way to turn a skateboard, it makes sense that the more lean you can put into a turn the sharper it will be. Flex will allow you to do just that.

There's no rule for determining the amount of flex that best suits a particular rider, a particular terrain, or performance in a particular fashion. Possibly more than any other aspect of skateboards, flex is a personal thing. Whether you want a board that will bend like a strip of sheet metal or one that you really have to get down on can only be discovered by experimentation. The only advice that can guide you is: pay close attention to how the board responds when you unweight. Sometimes referred to as "snap" or "punch," the board's ability to follow you immediately as you rise is vital. Unfortunately this property can't be measured in any kind of objective way. It's just something you'll have to pick up through trial and error.

Just as with stiff boards, there are disadvantages with flex. (Don't ever let anyone tell you that one is better than the other; it's strictly a matter of taste.) First, a flex board is a bit more difficult to get used to than a stiff board. Your first reaction when you mount a flex board will probably be, "How can I hold my balance riding when I can't even stand still on it?" Of course this feeling is only temporary, and won't last past the early learning stages. Linked to this is the obvious disadvantage of flex boards in high-speed runs. While other factors do contribute to "high-speed wobble," a flex board is more likely to react unfavorably than a stiff board under high-speed conditions. The reason behind this is the very same thing that makes a flex board smoother over rough surfaces. At reduced speeds flex will absorb shock without upsetting your equilibrium. But at thirty miles an hour plus, every deformity in the board's surface will be exaggerated. It's almost a chain reaction effect: each successive flexion builds on the next until the board is completely out of control.

Finally, a flex board has a more limited life span than a stiff board in terms of retaining its original shape. While a stiff board is more likely to break under an extreme impact, a flex board will eventually begin to lose its snap and begin to sag. This could take years, depending on the amount of skating you do, but it is a possibility.

The second way to classify boards is by the material used in their construction. The most popular are wood, fiberglass, plastic, aluminum, and fiberglass/wood laminations. Less used, but available, are rubber, Plexiglas, and Lexan.

In a way it's kind of silly to talk about stiff boards and then go on to talk about wood boards (see figure 2-a) because stiff boards are made of wood. But the quality of the wood and the nature of stiffness are really two entirely different things. Any wood will provide a stiff surface for a board, but not all wood will make a good stiff board.

2a   A good hard wood with a tight linear grain and a hard texturized finish is essential for safety and durability.

The most important factor in determining what kind of wood is best for a skateboard is hardness. There are plenty of good hard timbers available; unfortunately, most of them are very expensive. Ash, birch, and oak seem to be about the most practical. In addition to their resistance to breakage, these woods will hold truck mounting screws more securely.

You'll also want to take note of the grain. First make sure the grain is linear, that is, that it runs the length of the board. Also look for dark streaks in the grain. These indicate the points of greatest strength. A dark, linear grain will assure you that under normal weather and riding conditions the board won't warp.

A good hard finish on the board, such as urethane, mixed with sand (or otherwise texturized) is necessary. A slick deck can spell trouble on even a mild ride. If you find a board that meets all your requirements except this one, however, strips of grip tape are available at a minimal price. Although it will eventually peel up off the board, it's inexpensive to replace and will provide a more than adequate surface under any conditions.

Wood laminations will probably become an area of increasing interest in the near future. Some linear laminations (strips of wood glued together side by side) are available, but you'll want to steer clear of these. Breakage along the glue lines is a persistent problem; the only thing in this board's favor, therefore, is its visual appeal. The improved laminations will be of a dual-direction type, both linear and horizontal. Presumably, this type of board will provide a snappier flex with a longer life span. For the time being, though, good flex in a short board (twenty to thirty inches) can best be found in either fiberglass laminations or wood/fiberglass-combination laminates.

2b The most important thing to consider when buying a fiber glass board is how well it responds to your weighting and un-weighting. The only way to determine this is by getting on the board and trying it out.

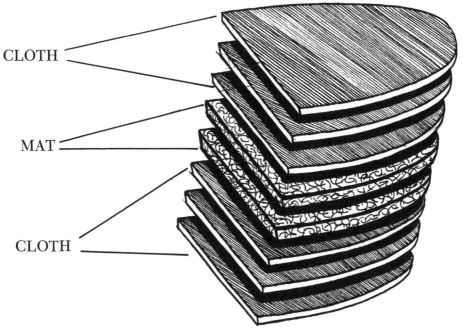

CLOTH

MAT

CLOTH

2c Not all hand-layed-up laminations are constructed this way, but this is a basic format. Resin is applied to each layer for adherance.

Right now, fiberglass (see figure 2-b) is dominating the skateboard market. Basically, fiberglass boards can be broken down into three main classes: hand–laid up, pultruded, and pressure laminations. These terms may appear somewhat technical, but they're actually pretty simple to grasp if you understand the basic laminating process.

Fiberglass laminations consist of two elements: some form of fiberglass (woven cloth, mat, or unidirectional glass strands) and epoxy resin. Layers of the fiberglass materials (in any combination) are alternated with coats of the epoxy resin. The epoxy is essentially a plastic glue, so the end result is something like a fiberglass sandwich that's cemented together. The advantages of such a composition are durability, resistance to breakage, and relatively good flex properties.

Some question exists as to which of the fiberglass materials is best suited to skateboard fabrication. There are those who insist the more woven cloth utilized in the board the more responsive the flex. Others feel the same way about unidirectional fiberglass strands. Some maintain that either form is acceptable. Nonetheless, experts usually agree that the mat substance (a type of cloth resembling paper) is the least preferable.

Hand–laid up laminations (see figure 2-c) usually consist of cloth and mat. Unidirectional fiberglass is never used in hand laminations. The process involves laying down a sheet of mat or cloth, usually about four by eight feet. Epoxy resin is then spread over the sheet and another layer of fiberglass is placed on top of it. Excess resin is squeezed out and the process is repeated until the desired thickness is reached. The lamination is then cured (hardened) either under heat or at room temperature. After the curing stage, the boards are sawed out of the laminate from a design called the template. Once the board is sanded and the holes drilled for truck mounting, the product is almost ready to use.

One of the most important things to remember about fiberglass boards is that the more glass used in the lamination in relation to resin, the snappier the flex. Because resin is squeezed out of a hand–laid up lamination manually, there's always more of it in the finished product than with the other laminations. This is the downfall of this type of board. What's worse, because human beings are not as precise as machines, there's no accurate way of knowing just how much resin is going to be left in the laminate. The task of judging the board therefore becomes somewhat more difficult. A rule of thumb is to check carefully for white flecks in the board. This is usually an indication that there is an overabundance of resin.

Probably the most common method of fiberglass board lamination is pultrusion, and it's also probably the best. As opposed to hand–laid up, pultrusion is strictly a mechanical process. A bit more complex, but in the long run it's cheaper and makes for a snappier board.

The operation begins with rolls of fiberglass material (cloth, mat, or unidirectional strands can be used). The materials are simultaneously pulled off the rolls in alternating layers and brought into a resin bath. The resin-soaked fiberglass then runs through a die. You can visualize the die if you place your hands together, leaving a small gap between your palms. The fiberglass would enter at the tips of your fingers and be brought through. The gap between the surfaces of the die is the exact thickness of the board. At the same time as resin is being squeezed out, heat coming through the die partially cures the laminate. It is then run through a long oven and fully cured.

As you can see, the amount of resin squeezed out is not only greater but standardized due to the precision of the die. The result is not only a better flexing board, but a board with better memory—that is, the property of returning to its original shape after being flexed. Constant tension on the laminate as it's pulled through the various stages also contributes to this quality. Bahne, one of the first pultruded boards, is about 60 percent glass, 40 percent resin. Although the ratio can be as great as 70 percent to 30 percent, the Bahne proportion is very good.

Most pultruded boards are of about the same quality. The important thing is the difference in glass-to-resin ratio. It's a good thing to inquire about when you're considering a particular board, but you'll probably have to write to the manufacturer to get the information.

Pressure-laminated boards are relatively rare, even though the process is relatively simple. Sheets of fiberglass material, presoaked in resin and partially cured, are laid up and laminated under heat and pressure.

Fiberglass/wood lamination (see figure 2-d) results in a board with both stability and snappy flex. The Gordon and Smith Fibreflex is a prime ex-

2d   A wood/fiber glass lamination gives you the best of both worlds — durability and responsive flex.

2e   A plastic board may give an approximate sensation of flex, but it's only an approximation. Basically a sag board, it's unsuited for a skater whose weight exceeds about 125 lbs.

ample of such a board. Both unidirectional fiberglass and cloth are incorporated into this board, along with two layers of maple veneer. The wood-veneer layers add an extra degree of flex and stability to the board. Glass content in the Fibreflex is purported to be 70 percent plus, undoubtedly an added advantage over most fiberglass boards. The only apparent drawback is cost, which is somewhere in the vicinity of 25 dollars for the board, minus trucks and wheels.

Another common material used for boards is plastic (see figure 2-e), usually polypropylene, polyolefin or ABS plastic; the properties of each are almost identical. The process most often used to create the shape of the board is injection molding, whereby the liquid plastic is squirted into a closed mold and cured, in much the same way many skateboard wheels and other plastic products are made.

Plastic boards are often referred to as "sag boards" because of their tendency to bow when you stand on them. Although a plastic board gives the sensation of flex, no true flexing takes place. The material simply will not follow you as you unweight. Plastic boards are very rugged and, because of the fabrication process, the nose and/or tail of the board can be turned up during manufacturing. Other boards can have these "kick nose" and "kick tail" variations (features that make certain tricks easier to perform), but you find them mostly on plastic or aluminum models. In addition to these benefits, plastic boards are inexpensive and can be a good investment when learning to ride or for getting a taste of flex.

The longer a plastic board, the more it will sag and the less responsive you'll find it. Stay with a short board of about twenty-four inches if you decide to go with plastic, and check for adequate support reinforcement on the underside of the board. Also keep in mind that polypropylene tends to stretch, and when stress is applied, mounting screws may work loose. The best type of mount for a plastic board, then, is a bolt that extends through the board and is locked on the surface with a nut and countersunk.

(One word of caution: if you weigh more than 125 pounds, stay away from plastic. The heavier you are, the more the board will sag and stay sagged.)

2f   Another semi-flex board, aluminum is durable, flashy but not really the most responsive piece of equipment.

2g   Rubber (above) and plexiglass are two substances that just aren't adaptable to skateboards. Despite manufacturers' claims, rubber and plexiglass offer nothing to the serious skater.

Aluminum boards (see figure 2-f) seem to be gaining in popularity these days, but it's more a matter of their novelty and flashy appearance than quality. That is not to say that aluminum's bad, but there are better materials. Aluminum will give you a fairly smooth ride with a small amount of flex. But, as with plastic, aluminum flex is only an approximation of the real thing. It's better than plastic, but not by that much—and it's more expensive.

The chief advantage of aluminum is its durability. Except for an occasional scratch, you're going to have a pretty tough time inflicting any real damage on an aluminum board. The only hazard involved is the tendency of the board's rails to sharpen as it's banged up on concrete. You can

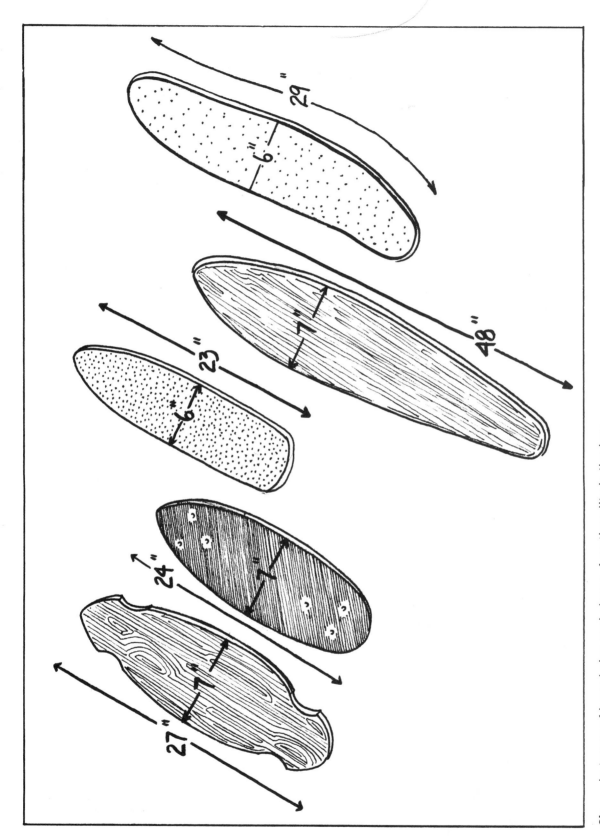

2h In terms of board size and shape, functionality is the key word. (left to right) Wheel well board, standard length wide board, standard length and width, long board and camber board.

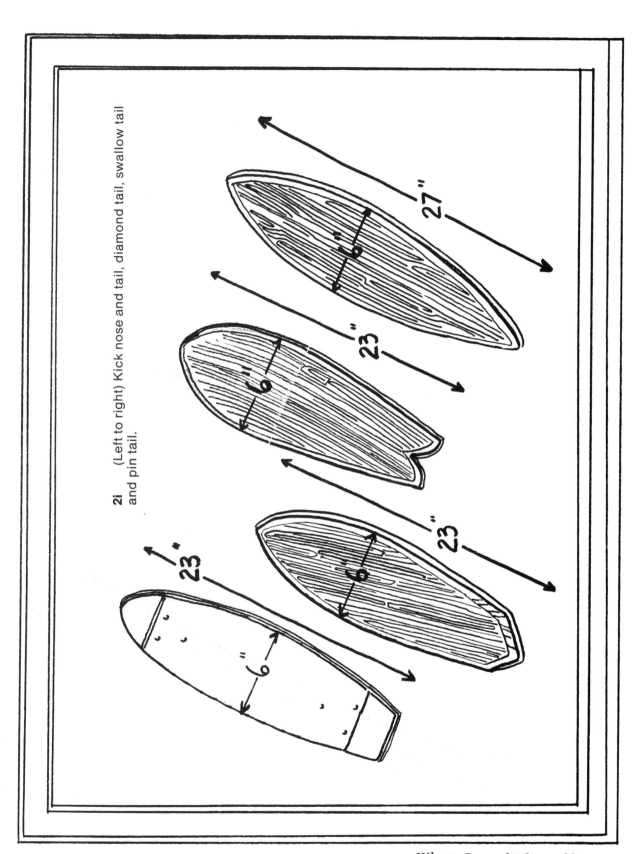

2i (Left to right) Kick nose and tail, diamond tail, swallow tail and pin tail.

imagine what would happen to your legs if one of those razor-sharp edges were to catch you in a spin-out. Periodic filing of the rails will lessen that possibility, but it's still extra maintenance.

Lowest on the list of boards are those made of rubber, Plexiglas, or any material resembling either (see figure 2-g). Rubber is very durable, but its weight and total lack of flex make it undesirable. Plexiglas is also heavy and inflexible and, what is more, it's extremely brittle and likely to crack and chip before long. Unless you're out to lose money, don't even consider either material.

Finally there are size and shape to consider (see figures 2h and 2-i). In terms of length, the formula is simple: the shorter the board, the better the turning efficiency and degree of maneuverability; the longer the board, the more stability at high speeds and the more similarity in riding style to surfing. On a short board of around twenty-four to twenty-eight inches, with good, grippy wheels and high-performance trucks, you can execute sharp turns more easily, including the 180- and 360-degree turns we'll look at later in the book. Although most tricks can be performed on a long board (some reach four feet six inches in length), if you're not experienced in freestyle, a shorter board will probably respond more accurately to your body movements. But for high speeds, long boards are a necessity and, except for the most experienced skater, anyone who surpasses twenty miles an hour on a short board is begging for blood.

When looking at a board for shape, keep in mind that what you want is something practical, not something that has eye appeal. A fairly blunt nose will withstand impact better than a sharp one, and a broad, rounded tail will give better leverage and offer more room to move in freestyle-type riding. Besides, if you're going to get into tail wheelies and radical turns, any shape variation in the tail will be altered as the board drags on the concrete. Pin tails, swallow tails, diamond tails, and the like serve no purpose other than the visual, and any sharp lines will eventually manage to bang up against your leg. For a short board, a width of six inches or so at the widest point is ideal; about seven inches for a long board. These seem to be the optimum widths for stability and maneuverability.

As mentioned before, the kick tail and kick nose are common shape variations. For tricks that require leverage, these are really helpful. Unfortunately, most boards incorporating these features are made of the less desirable materials.

Another variation is the wheel well. With longer axles and wider wheels being used more and more frequently, you may find that in executing radical turns which involve extreme leaning the board will actually graze the wheels. When this happens, forward motion will stop suddenly and you'll be thrown from the board. Routed wells on the underside of the board above each wheel will increase the clearance, and a semicircular cut above each wheel will give you total freedom in these circumstances.

A feature that you'll probably be seeing more and more of is camber.

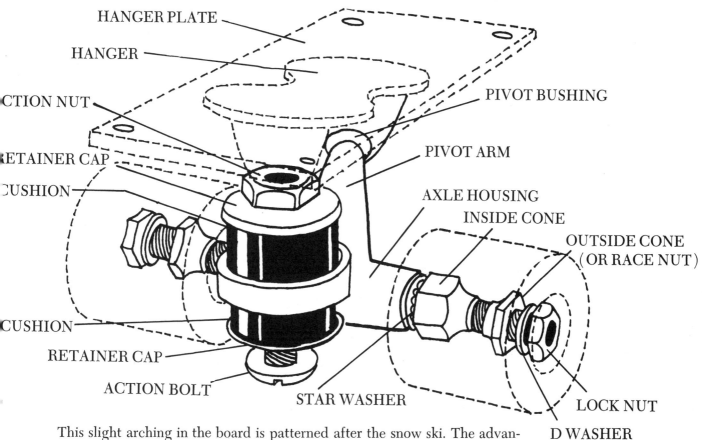

HANGER PLATE

HANGER

CTION NUT

RETAINER CAP

CUSHION

CUSHION

RETAINER CAP

ACTION BOLT

STAR WASHER

PIVOT BUSHING

PIVOT ARM

AXLE HOUSING

INSIDE CONE

OUTSIDE CONE
(OR RACE NUT)

LOCK NUT

D WASHER

This slight arching in the board is patterned after the snow ski. The advantage here is that standing on the board actually flattens it, rather than causing it to sag downward. What this produces is just about the ideal amount of flex. The board is tight and controllable, with excellent memory and responsiveness.

Gimmickry is unavoidable when a particular item becomes hot on the market. Manufacturers, aware that we all like to be unique if not best, will often jump at new variations, which are frequently useless and sometimes self-defeating. Shapes that have no apparent justification other than their uniqueness should be ignored. The best thing to do when you're considering any aspect of any product is to ask yourself, "Why did the manufacturer make this change?" If there's no practical reason, laugh it off and leave it for the sucker. A skateboard should be a completely functional thing: meaningless trimmings are, well, just meaningless trimmings.

Trucks

Although the truck may appear to be nothing more than a hunk of metal and rubber that houses the axle, it is actually a precision part that's critical to the performance of the board (see figure 2-j). Essentially the truck is a suspension device that can either enhance or impair shock absorption and turning mobility, depending on quality.

For a long time skateboard trucks were identical to showtype roller skate trucks. It didn't take long, though, for riders and manufacturers alike to realize that, despite the similarity in function, roller skate trucks just weren't performing adequately for skateboards. Again, the problem was related to the fact that roller skating involves two independent pieces of equipment and that achieving traction, stability, and turning efficiency is a different process when two separate sets of wheels are involved. First of all, roller skate trucks use only one rubber cushion between where the truck is mounted to the skate and the axle. The result is a limiting of side-to-side action, which anyone who's been on roller skates knows is necessary to maintain stability. Second, the cushions are made of urethane or other hard, rubbery substances. This is all right for roller skating because to absorb shock you can lift your leg up and the skate will follow. Not so on a skateboard. Both feet being on the board, shock caused by riding over a less than smooth surface is transferred more readily up through your legs.

The need, then, was for a truck that utilized two softer cushions to absorb shock and improve turning capacity. The demand was fulfilled quickly, both by standard roller skate truck manufacturers and newcomers to the field.

There are several variations in common skateboard trucks now on the market. Probably the most basic is in the type of material used in the cushions. Urethane and rubber dominate the field, but for all intents and purposes, rubber is better. The reason is simply that rubber is softer. Although urethane can be produced in ideal durometer (degree of hardness) for wheels, the truck requires a spongier material for the reasons stated above. Rubber will generally wear more quickly and will eventually deteriorate beyond the point of efficiency, but at 25 cents apiece, replacement shouldn't be a cause for concern. When checking into trucks, remove a cushion and squeeze it between your thumb and index finger. The hole through which the action bolt runs should oval out easily if not flatten out altogether. If you're not satisfied with the cushions but find the truck to your liking in other ways, ask the salesman to replace them with a different set. Another rule of thumb is, the bigger the cushion (up to a point), the more the truck will respond overall.

Size is another variable. Most trucks are made of aluminum, and weight is of little concern. So make sure the one you purchase has a truck which is beefy both in the axle housing and pivot arm. Axle length varies, usually ranging from about four to nine inches. The trend, however, is toward longer and longer ones which will increase board stability, especially on a fast run. Being a relatively recent development, it's not clear yet whether maneuverability is negatively affected. You'll be safe within the four to nine inch range, but past that you'll be experimenting.

Axles also vary in diameter: they are either 5/16 or 9/32 of an inch. Most are 5/16, and these are generally better. Although the 1/32 of an inch difference might not seem like much, the added thickness will make for a more rugged axle. Cones and locknuts are not interchangeable between the two diameters.

Also in terms of size, it's important to note the height of the truck. The ideal here will be determined largely by the diameter of the wheel you'll be riding on. The lower the truck, the lower the center of gravity and the greater the degree of overall mobility. But a big wheel mounted on a truck that's too short will rub against the bottom of the board. Also make sure the head of the action bolt doesn't hang lower than the axle housing. Certain tricks and changes from sloped to flat ground can cause the bolt head to scrape on the ground. At best this will slow you down. At worst, it might bring your board to a sudden stop, pitching you off unexpectedly. Many manufacturers ignore this factor and, as a result, the market is flooded with trucks having this deficiency. Many of these boards are outstanding in every other way, but clearance between the ground and the action bolt head is critical and should be checked out carefully.

The hanger plate is another area you should investigate thoroughly. Most are metal, but a durable plastic such as that used in the Bennett Flexhanger won't detract from the board's flex properties. A plate that will accommodate four mounting screws is also desirable. This feature, along with abundant surface area, will safeguard against mounting screws ripping out of the board.

Shock absorption pads placed between the hanger plate and board are becoming a common modification. These spongy pads reduce shock, but they also reduce the degree to which the board reacts to your movements. The general rule is that the more things placed between the source of power (in this case you) and the machine (the truck and wheels), the less efficient the entire system becomes. The same applies to elevator pads, which unfortunately are sometimes necessary to accommodate larger wheels. If you must elevate the board from the truck or add shock-absorbing material, make sure it's as thin as possible and made of urethane as opposed to rubber. The stiffer urethane will reduce to some extent the degree to which the pad interferes with the board's responsiveness.

Other details you should inspect include the straightness of the axle bore. Simply make sure the openings through which the axle runs on either side of the housing are in exactly the same spot on both sides. An opening which is even slightly out of line with the other will greatly impair the board's efficiency. While you're at it, take the axle out and roll it along a flat surface to make sure it's straight. Also make certain that there's a bushing in the pivot socket of the hanger. Many hangers don't have one and the metal-to-metal contact between the pivot arm and the socket can create a rough ride.

Cones (or race nuts as they're often called) should also be inspected for imperfections in the metal. You'll want a smooth surface so that the ball bearings will race around the cone uniformly. As a final check of the truck's quality, be certain there's a star washer between the axle housing and the inside cone. Its absence may indicate that the manufacturer has cut corners in other areas of the truck.

Locknuts and hanger plate mounting nuts should be of the nylon insert type. This type of nut is coated on the inside with a nylon plastic which will resist loosening. Should the nut for some reason begin to untighten, it will probably do so slowly enough that you'll detect it during routine maintenance, before it gets very far along.

An innovation to keep your eye out for is "spring-mounted trucks." Some exist now but they are still inadequate. The idea of incorporating springs into the suspension of a skateboard is logical, but a lot more work will be required to perfect it. Independent wheel systems, i.e., those with a separate axle for each wheel, will also be surfacing soon. Again, it's a good idea, but we'll have to wait to see whether it's developed properly.

Wheels

Wheels have come a long since the days of clay composition. Right now you can get a wheel to suit just about any riding condition and some that will function well under all conditions. As mentioned, urethane has been the most significant development in skateboard wheels. By manipulating the durometer of the urethane, varying degrees of traction can be achieved. It would be difficult to be specific about ideal durometer, but it's a fact that the harder the wheel, the less the traction but the faster the ride. Don't be deceived by this generalization, however. Even a soft wheel will give you the capacity to achieve speeds that would probably be best left unattempted. Only if you're going for the speed record (which, by the way, is held by Denis Schufeldt, who was clocked at about fifty miles an hour) should you think about a harder wheel.

Urethane wheels can be produced in any of three ways. Pour molding, as the name implies, involves literally pouring the liquid urethane into a mold and then curing it slowly. Durometer is harder to control in a pour-molding situation and the result is a wheel that's usually softer and more flexible, with a better memory, but also one which occasionally has slight imperfections in its shape.

Injection molding (the same process used in injection-molded plastic boards), on the other hand, produces a harder wheel for the most part. The process is cheaper and in some ways less satisfactory. For instance, because races (the dishlike metal part of the wheel in which the bearings run) can't be set into an injection-molded wheel as quickly as a pour-molded one, the bond between the race and the wheel often isn't as strong. As the injection-molded wheel heats up with use, it expands and can pull away from the race. A wheel with this tendency may eventually pop the race out altogether.

A third method of fabrication is pressure molding. Here the urethane is also poured into a mold but, in contrast to pour molding, a cap is placed on the open end of the mold and pressed down. The major advantage of this process is that the races can be molded directly into the wheel and durometer can be controlled more easily.

Next to the introduction of urethane, the greatest advance in wheel technology has been the introduction of the precision bearing. But first let's look at the most prevalent type: the loose ball bearing wheel (see figure 2-k).

Every loose-ball wheel requires sixteen bearings (eight on either side), set loosely in the wheel's races. The cone nuts are then placed over the race, creating the encasement in which the bearings run. Loose-ball wheels are cheaper than precision-bearing ones (about $1 to $5), but there are several disadvantages.

First, a loose-ball wheel must be broken down and cleaned periodically. Because the bearings are largely exposed, dirt collects in the races and, unless the whole assembly (bearings, races and cones) is cleaned, the wheel won't turn freely. Second, loose-ball wheels are a lot louder than precision. Third, although there's still some argument about it, loose-ball wheels are generally considered rougher riding and less exact than precision wheels. Finally, there is always a chance that for one reason or another (heat expansion and stress on the inner wheel are two possible causes) the races will pop out of the wheel.

2k   Most common of the skateboard wheels, the loose-ball bearing wheel performs well but requires constant adjustment.

2l Precision bearings will probably take over the skateboard
wheel market in due time. They're quieter, require no adjustment
and may very well prove to be more high performance.

Precision-bearing wheels (see figure 2-l) are by no means new, they're
just new to skateboarding. Used in a variety of things from automotive
machinery to vacuum cleaners, precision-bearing units look like little disks
about one-half of an inch in diameter. As you can see, the bearings are
packed with lubricant and set in the disk, which in turn is inserted into the
wheel. The spacer (in the foreground of the picture) sits between the bearing units and maintains the proper distance and parallelism between them.
Cones, races, and D washers are unnecessary.

Some precision bearings, such as the ones pictured, are partially shielded,
while others are fully encased so that the balls are not exposed to dirt.

The precision-bearing wheel requires no maintenance whatsoever and is
quieter and more accurate in its spin. It is also about twice as expensive as
the loose-bearing type and, other than the reduction in noise and frequency
of maintenance, the difference in performance is not readily detectable by
an inexperienced skater.

A third bearing type, the self-contained assembly (see figure 2-m), incorporates features of both the loose- and precision-type wheels. Races are
utilized in the wheels, but when compared with the loose-bearing wheel,
they are less dished-out and somewhat flatter in appearance. However, in
place of the cone nuts, a two-part unit composed of a female and longer

male component is substituted. The male portion is run through the wheel and the bearings are set between its conelike section and the race. The female portion is then placed in the other side and the bearings dropped in as they were on the male side. The two parts are then snapped together and the wheel mounted to the truck like the loose-ball type.

2m   The male section of the self-contained bearing unit (left) is also a built-in spacer and eliminates the need for cone adjustment.

The wheels then function in the same way as the loose-bearing variety but, because the cones are prespaced by the length of the male portion, cone adjustment is eliminated. Self-contained bearings must still be cleaned periodically, but the process is simplified in the reassembly stage.

This concept has been around for a while, but earlier versions were made of poor alloys. As a result, the self-contained unit had a tendency to separate with wear. Newer ones, however, seem to remain intact despite frequent use and perform as well as loose-ball wheels.

The size and shape of the wheel (see figure 2-n) are also very important. And this is where personal preference comes into play, more so than with any other aspect of skateboard wheels. The type of terrain skated, the speed and degree of traction desired, as well as the size of the rider should all be considered when deciding on a wheel.

The standard wheel is approximately 1¼ inches wide by 2 inches in diameter. Many skaters believe it has totally outlived its usefulness. Others argue that it's the most maneuverable. If it is (and that's not certain), the difference is minute. Outweighing any possible additional maneuverability

2n (Left to right) The super wide wheel, flex wheel, "Stoker-size" wheel, racing slick and standard wheel.

is the lack of traction exhibited by this wheel. For freestyle, downhill, and slalom skating, traction is essential and this wheel affords very little.

The racing slick is a popular wheel and for its size (about 1½ inches wide by 1¾ inches in diameter) has good traction due to its tapered edge. But when it comes to speed, it's not much better than the standard wheel.

The "Stoker-size" wheel (so named for the original manufacturer), which measures about two inches by two inches, is a vast improvement over the standard wheel. Faster because it's higher, it also provides additional traction and is more efficient over rough terrain.

The concept of a flex wheel is an excellent one. Varying in size, the flexible lip offers good traction. However, since flex wheels are only tapered on one side, their full potential is not being utilized. As with all bigger wheels, a small rider can't apply enough weight to the entire wheel to get full traction. This is a particular problem with flex wheels. Watch for new versions that will come in varying wall thicknesses and be tapered on both sides of the wheel.

Finally we get to the super-wide wheels which are about two inches in diameter by about three inches in width. Traction is obviously superior with these wheels, but maneuverability is often reduced. In addition, most axles aren't made to accommodate such a wheel and the stress applied by the extreme width can be enough to bend the axle.

Judging the quality of a particular wheel can be a tricky thing, but there are a few guidelines. When inspecting a loose-ball design, roll the wheel along a flat surface, watching the races carefully. If they're not parallel to each other, you'll notice a wobbling-in-and-out effect in the wheel. You'll obviously want to avoid such a wheel. Also avoid plastic races. As with any component, if you haven't the money to get a good wheel (wheels with plastic races are the least expensive), wait and save up. Plastic races are a definite break-and-replace proposition.

Both loose-ball and precision-bearing wheels should be inspected for symmetry and traction. Roll them around, rub them over a surface, and, if you can, try a board with the kind of wheels you're interested in.

Presence of air bubbles and dark spots is also a sign that the wheel might not perform up to par.

Finally, determine what kind of ball bearings come with the wheel. Grades of 100, 200, 500, and 1000 indicate the accuracy of the roundness with 100 being the best.

SAFETY: 3 PRACTICES AND EQUIPMENT

THERE'S NO QUESTION about it: if you ride a skateboard, you're going to fall from time to time. And, while skateboarding is less expensive and more accessible than surfing and skiing, that's not snow or water beneath you. This is not to say you're eventually going to wind up in a serious accident, however. On the contrary, if you keep your wits about you, ride defensively, and equip yourself properly, chances are that even if you do fall you won't be badly hurt.

The most basic safety consideration is making sure the area you plan to skate is safe. Since most skating is done on the road or sidewalk, the first thing to check out is traffic and pedestrian flow. Without going very far, just about anyone can find an area that, if not totally free of cars and pedestrians, is relatively quiet. In skateboarding, enough is already demanded of the rider physically, without bringing other factors into the picture. Inanimate obstacles are bad enough, but things that move, like people and cars, vastly increase the risk of collision.

A relatively unused part of a school yard is an ideal location (see figure 3-a). Without cars, animals, or package-laden pedestrians, it's just you and

3a   This wall, approximately six feet high, curves around half the yard at a junior high school in Los Angeles. Safe and challenging, such areas are ideal for skating.

the skateboard. And if you look at a school yard in terms of skating terrain, you may be pleasantly surprised to find that many were designed with nicely banked walls, ramps, and smooth surfaces.

If you have to stick to the streets, pay careful attention to the slope of the terrain. Many hills are deceptive in this respect. If it's constant even a relatively mild gradient can propel you at top speeds. Make sure the surface is sufficiently smooth and free of large cracks, bumps, and debris. Also, if the area you're skating is a slope, be certain you'll have enough room to stop at the bottom without drifting into traffic or crashing into walls or fences.

Skateboard parks would really be the best (see figure 3-b), but, for the most part, the idea is still in the dream stages. A couple do, however, exist. While these areas may not be the most challenging spots, they're definitely safer. Carefully-designed, the skateboard park could be almost totally safe, both for the rider and the general public. The catch comes in getting one laid out and constructed. A private company could do it (some may), but the most realistic approach to securing an inexpensive, if not free, park is through local government.

As skateboarding grows, the threat to all concerned also grows, unfortunately. On the whole, local governments have responded in only a negative way: they have banned the sport in some or all parts of the city. It's logical; if something poses a problem, eliminate it. But it's obviously not the only possible course of action. Isolating the activity in a predetermined, intelligently designed area will satisfy everyone. Getting it done, though, requires hard work.

Lobbying is the key to the solution. If you're interested in creating a skateboard park, you're going to have to organize and prepare for action. This will undoubtedly involve writing letters, attending city council and parks and recreation department meetings, and putting together petition drives. A group from one southern California community actually produced a film depicting the problems faced both by skateboarders and citizens. The film was presented to the city council along with plans for a park.

3b   Establishing the Ventura Skateboard Park in Ventura, Calif. took a co-operative community effort. Rather tame, it's a good spot for learning and casual skating.

The most important thing is demonstrating a need, and that means grouping with fellow riders en masse. No local government official with any sense is going to embark upon a project that may cost a few thousand dollars for the sake of a handful of disgruntled skaters. And be prepared for hassles arising over insurance and land use. These are common obstacles, but ones that can be worked out if you're armed with the facts.

"Tune Your Board"

"An untuned car means trouble." Remember that advertising slogan? Well, the same applies to your skateboard. There isn't a thing you can do to prevent accidents if your board isn't in shape. Keep in mind that the skateboard is really an extension of your own body. You wouldn't skate with a broken ankle and you shouldn't skate with a board that isn't tuned and adjusted for the kind of riding you're going to do. As mentioned in Chapter Two, for a fast downhill run, a longer, stable board is essential. Whether you use one or not, at least make sure the trucks are well tightened to reduce high-speed wobbling and wandering of the board.

Always check the wheel locknuts for tightness, as well as the hanger plate mounting nuts. Sanding splintered glass or wood is also necessary to injury-free skating. If you use grip tape on your board, see to it that it's adhering fully to the surface. Curled-up edges can trip you up, especially in freestyle skating. If you're not using grip tape, you probably should be.

As for safety equipment, ask yourself this question, "Would a 200-pound halfback stand up to a 270-pound defensive tackle without a helmet and pads?" The answer is obvious. Football pads were designed for a reason: the contact nature of the sport demanded it. Let me tell you, though, the concrete below you is infinitely harder than any football player's body. On top of that, you can run around a tackle, but you can't run from cement.

Safety equipment specifically designed for skateboarding is relatively scarce, even though more is becoming available. But there are plenty of adequate substitutes. You may not find a whole lot of skaters taking these precautions, but most of the best do. First of all, wear a shirt and long pants if you're going to be doing any kind of risky skating. For some skaters, that might mean a forty mile an hour downhill run; for some it might mean an occasional tail or nose wheelie. Only you know how far you're extending yourself, and you should know how to protect yourself. If you have any doubt at all, use your head and don't be swayed by what you see others doing. Tennis shoes (preferably high-top for ankle support), knee and elbow pads, and gloves all offer good protection.

Equipment

For high-speed skating, a helmet is mandatory (see figure 3-c). If you don't have enough smarts to wear one, cracking your skull open might not

3c   High speed runs demand a helmet, gloves, shirt, long pants and shoes. Helmets are pretty expensive but you may be able to pick one up cheap in a second-hand store.

affect the functioning of your brain (you'd already have hit bottom on the intelligence scale), but it will sure mess up your looks, if that's what's important to you. Actually, since most serious skateboard accidents are inflicted on the skull, a helmet is a good idea any time, but for speeds of over twenty miles an hour, you've got to wear one.

The ideal helmet is one that's lightweight, yet sturdy, well ventilated, and well padded. Ear holes are also a good idea. Very few skateboard helmets exist at the present time but other types will fit the bill. Football, hockey, or motorcycle helmets usually conform to a skater's needs. If you buy a helmet, expect to pay around $25 or $30. It's definitely an investment, and a wise one.

One of the advances in the area of skateboard safety equipment is the impact jacket or suit (see figure 3-d). Right now these are in the prototype stage, but if the idea catches on and the equipment is marketed, you should look into it. Impact equipment should fit snugly without being confining. It should adequately cover the bony, protruding parts of your body, such as shoulders, elbows, and knees, and should have heavy-duty nylon seams. You'll also want to make sure the garment is lightweight and well ventilated. Aside from proposed cost, this seems to be the major problem at the moment; if not well designed, impact equipment could really suffocate you.

Safety Begins Within

I've touched on the terrain, the board, and safety equipment; the next logical factor in this sequence is you, the skater. Safety begins and ends with you, within your mind and within your body. I could ramble on, quoting accident statistics, relating stories of gruesome falls and collisions, but the point should be clear without all that. Skateboarding is a dangerous sport unless you have it together mentally and physically. Denis Schufeldt, a top-ranked skater, has actually applied principles of yoga to skateboarding in an effort to bring mind and body together as one integrated, totally functioning unit. What is important to remember here is that, as in all athletic endeavors, skateboarding involves a total harmony of mind and body.

On a simple level, safe skating hinges on this cooperation between body and mind. There is a very thin line between accepting challenge and wisely backing off. This division is something no one can teach you; you must be aware of your physical limitations, and learn at what point you

3d   High proposed retail cost and lack of consumer interest put an end to production of this impact suit. As you can see, such a garment would afford ideal protection. The idea should, and probably will, be developed in the very near future.

can go no farther. This is the essence of safe riding, remaining within the bounds of your physical limits. Deciding how far this limit can extend requires a constant awareness of why you're doing a particular thing and how far it is from what you've already done. More than just not taking ridiculous chances, you'll have to adopt an attitude of patience with, and consideration of, your life and limbs.

Avoid the "Evel Knievel syndrome." Unless you become a highly skilled skater, don't let your mind keep crying out "More!" This involves keeping not only freestyle skating within realistic bounds, but high-speed as well—in fact, especially high-speed. Somebody once suggested to me that skaters who shoot for maximum speed do so only because they can't perform in any other way. I don't know if I'm ready to go that far, but it's something to keep in mind. A possible rule for maximum safety would be: Never exceed the speed at which you can successfully jump off the board.

Other rules to keep in mind: (1) Don't cling to cars while on your board. Even at reduced speeds this is extremely dangerous. The slightest variation in the driving pattern or road (not to mention your own control) can drag you under the wheels of the car. (2) Look behind you frequently, especially when zigzagging across a road. Even on precision-bearing wheels your board will create noise. Compounded by wind whistle, it's more than likely you'll never hear a car coming up on you from behind unless the driver honks his horn. But for some reason, a lot of drivers seem to think that skateboarders have radarlike senses and try to avoid you without signaling with the horn. Any quick change of direction on your part can bring you face to face with a 4,000-pound car.

Finally, respect pedestrians and drivers. They are human beings just like you for whom you should have consideration. But if you want to look at it selfishly, they may be taxpayers and voters with enough potential clout to bring about the banning of skateboarding in your community. Every accident, every confrontation with a driver or pedestrian is another signature (or signatures) on the petition to suppress the sport.

Falling

I wouldn't be doing justice to the idea of skateboarding safety if I didn't go into some detail concerning falling. Falling is an important aspect of many sports and in particular the martial arts. Jeff Campbell, a physical education teacher and consultant to Hang Ten Sportboards, has written extensively on falling technique in *Skateboarder* magazine. What he has to say makes a lot of sense and should be taken to heart by any serious skater.

Campbell identifies mass and speed as the major factors affecting impact (in the case of skateboarding, the collision of your body and the ground). The force of impact is directly related to the mass of the falling object (for our purposes your weight) and the speed at which it falls. The less mass, or weight, the less damage upon impact. The same applies to speed. Of course you can't do much about your mass; the bigger you are the harder you'll fall. But you can reduce the speed of the fall by lowering your center of gravity just prior to the fall, thus reducing the distance between you and the ground and the speed at which you'll hit it.

Falling forward will most likely inflict injury to the hands, wrists, forearms, shoulders, and head. A backward fall will most seriously affect the back, spinal cord, hips, and buttocks. The ability of the body to absorb the force of the fall is the most controllable factor. So, outside of lowering your center of gravity, the first rule is: Fall so that the fleshier parts of your body absorb the impact.

"IMPACT ABSORPTION ROLL"

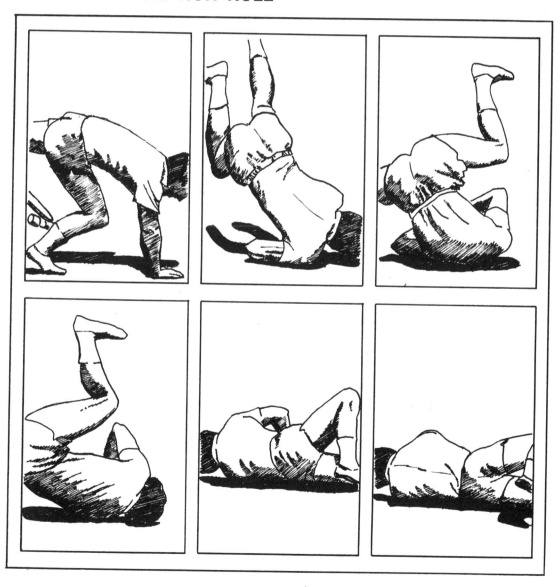

Second, impact can be reduced by distributing the force of the fall to many sections of the body. The longer the impact force is applied to a particular area of the body, the more damage done. So you'll want to distribute the force before it has been applied to any one part of the body for an extended period of time. The way to do this is by rolling at the moment of impact. In a forward-fall situation (see figure 3-e), first lower your center of gravity and then roll forward with your head turned away from the direction of the fall. Complete the roll with two or three sideway rolls. By following this pattern, you'll distribute the impact force from your forearm, to the back of your shoulders, to the opposite buttock, and down the upper thigh to the lower leg and foot.

In a backward-roll situation, reverse the sequence. Begin the roll with the fleshy part of the calf, moving to the upper part of the thigh, across the buttock to the opposite shoulder, with your head tucked in to your forearm. Extend the move with a few sideway rolls. Remember, both of these rolls differ from a somersault in that you're not rolling directly heels over head; by starting on one side and completing the roll on the opposite side, you are taking the impact diagonally across your body rather than on the bony areas, such as your head and spine. Also try to remain flexible. The first reaction to a fall is body tension, but allowing the limbs to spring slightly will further reduce impact force.

Above all, when you fall, don't try to break the impact by sliding. You'll literally whittle your hands and knees down.

I would strongly advise practicing these techniques before using them in an actual fall. And remember, the only thing better than knowing how to fall is keeping yourself out of falling situations.

THE ART

4

As with any skill, learning to skateboard won't happen all at once unless you have some unusual God-given talent for it. In fact, the kind of gliding motion that is the essence of skating is unnatural to the human body. You may very well fall on your rear end immediately the first time you get on a skateboard. Even if you do, eventual mastery is not out of the question by any means, for the fundamentals involved in the sport—balance, co-ordination, and ambition—are basic to most physical activities. Whether or not you have ever snow skied or surfed before, you've often put into practice the elements of skating. Physically, you must have some control over your body. Emotionally, you must have self-confidence and desire. These are the only prerequisites.

To begin, find a smooth, flat, vacant area, one where you aren't likely to encounter cars, pedestrians, or pets. It might be a good idea to bring along a friend especially one who knows something about skating. Any living body will do, however; what you need is a shoulder to lean on for balance and moral support. Your first encounter with the board shouldn't consist of anything more than just pedaling yourself around. If you're right-handed

54   The Skateboard Book

and kick a football with your right foot, place your right foot on the board just over the rear truck. When you feel secure in this position, push off with your left foot, slowly at first and then developing a little speed.

When you've gotten the hang of pushing off in this manner, bring your left foot onto the board. At this point, move your right foot up slightly toward the center of the board and your left foot back just a bit. Your weight center should be directly over the center of the board, so that your feet will probably be just inside of the trucks. Feet should be pointed at a 45-degree angle to the front of the board (see figure 4-a).

4a

The parallel stance, sometimes utilized in speed runs, is a variation of this basic position. Such a stance will allow you to get into the air-foil position (which I'll describe) more easily, but it will also impair your maneuverability and make jumping off the board, should you begin to lose control, much more difficult.

4b   Turning is simply a matter of leaning. Notice how the
angle of the lean here (about 45°) corresponds to the angle of
the wheels to the board.

During the glide, your elbows should be in toward your waist and your
hands just slightly forward. This stance will increase your balance. Keep
your knees bent just a bit for shock absorption, flexibility, and lowered
center of gravity. It's important that you not lean backward or forward in
this early stage. Leaning back (usually out of over cautiousness) or push-

ing your weight forward (usually out of overeagerness) will almost surely send you sprawling at this point in the learning process. Greatest stability is achieved by allowing all your weight to rest directly above your feet.

Glide around like this in straight lines for a while, pushing off periodically. Your primary concern at this point is to accustom your body to the sensation of forward momentum. As you become more confident, you might want to pump your body up and down slightly. However, don't force this or any other aspect of skateboarding. If your body says "No!", respect it.

Once you've developed the process of achieving forward motion to your satisfaction, you're ready to attempt turning (see figure 4-b). There's no secret to this. Turning is very simply a matter of leaning to the right for right turns and leaning to the left for left turns. The right foot is often considered the "drive foot," while the left is the "steering foot." Concentrate on this when leaning for a turn. Also remember that turning efficiency is largely a matter of how tight the trucks are. A tighter, less responsive truck is probably wise in the beginning, as your intent here isn't high performance but rather keeping your two feet on the board.

To begin a turn, lean your hips and upper body to the side of the desired turn. Keep your weight just slightly forward for balance and your knees slightly bent. Your elbows and hands should rest in toward your waist, as any additional upper-body movement will spoil your balance. If you rotate your shoulders in the direction of the turn, you'll probably lose your balance to the point of not being able to recover it again. The harder or farther your lean into a turn, the sharper it will be. To end the turn and regain a straight course, simply shift your weight back to the center of the board, hips first, followed by your upper body. Again, learning to gauge and execute turns must be a progressive thing. Take it gradually and increase the degree and speed of turns as you build skill and confidence.

Once you've fully mastered these basic techniques, you'll be ready to approach sloped and irregular terrains, as well as attempt freestyle, slalom, and downhill speed runs (if this is where your interest lies).

Slalom, in addition to being a competition event, can also be used under a variety of skating conditions. The idea in slalom is to maneuver your board through a series of obstacles that can be arranged either in a straight ("in line") or zigzagged ("switchback") configuration. Slalom events in snow-skiing competition utilize flags around which the skier moves. In skateboard slalom, cones are substituted for the flags. But on any downhill run, you can devise a series of imaginary obstacles through which to weave. For purposes of explanation, however, let's assume a course that is complete with cones.

Sudden directional change is the essence of slalom skating. Basically, envision a weaving line made up of repeated slight turns. These are accomplished by the same means described above for simple direction change. The only difference, of course, is that the turns follow each other quickly from side to side. The key to efficiency in slalom is the principle that the shortest distance between two points is a straight line. In other words, to attack a slalom course with accuracy and speed you must follow a path whose curves are as slight as you can make them, cutting as close to the cones as possible on both sides (see figure 4-c). The cleaner the line, or the line with the least turn severity, the faster you can execute the course.

In addition, every turn must be counterbalanced by a turn of equal sharpness. A smooth, balanced approach is essential to perfecting slalom technique. Each turn should also be accompanied by a synchronized pumping of the arms and shoulders.

Speed through a slalom course is also increased by proper weighting and unweighting. As mentioned before, this a process of pressing down on the board (weighting) and then rising up. Putting more weight on your foot while springing on the ball of your back foot as you weight into the cone and unweight coming out of it will propel you quickly and evenly around the cones.

Integral to slalom technique is minimization of upper-body movement. Any extraneous body movement will detract from your critical downhill momentum. Also, always think ahead; your every action must be directed toward what is approaching.

I'm very reluctant to get into downhill speed skating at all. Although it is attractive in some ways and there is a certain thrill factor involved, it's a very risky proposition. Speed skating is the primary cause of serious skateboarding injuries and, to an extent, it's a form of skating that is really incompatible with the nature of the sport. After all, even with safety equipment, you're virtually unprotected in a high-speed situation. The damage done to an automobile upon impact at ten miles an hour is incredible, and when you're talking about flesh and bones impacting at thirty, forty, or fifty miles an hour—well, it's frightening.

On the other hand, speed skating is a reality and, at the risk of arming you with a potentially deadly weapon, I feel compelled to pass along a few thoughts on the subject.

Aside from the condition of the board and the inclination of the run, air resistance is the primary factor in speed. A broader surface will be met by more air resistance in forward motion. You've probably experienced this while walking into the wind with an open umbrella. Another example: automobiles stacked high with packages in the rooftop luggage rack will get decreased gas mileage because the engine has to work harder to maintain the same speed.

For maximum speed, then, the skater must reduce his body surface in order to reduce air resistance. Of course, you can't shrink or poke holes in

4c   When executing a slalom run, keep in mind that the ideal line to follow is the straightest (here indicated by the solid line). The broken line represents a course that will reduce speed by increasing the area skated and by causing unnecessary body movement.

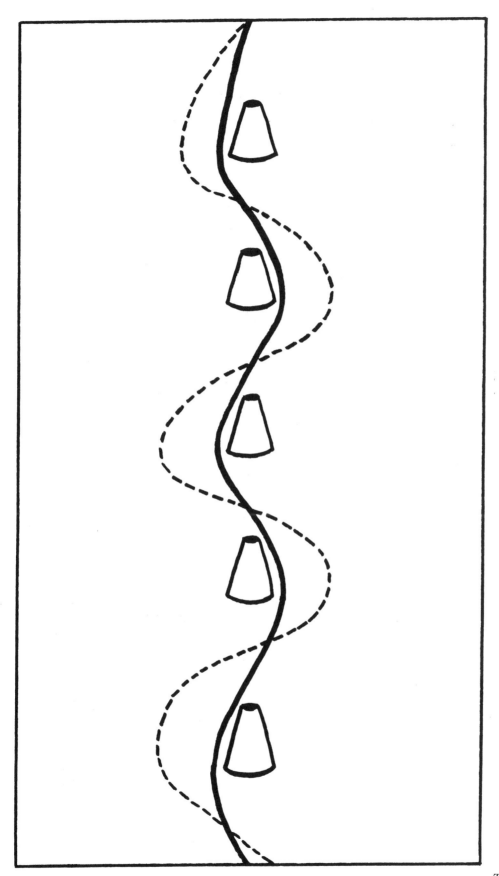

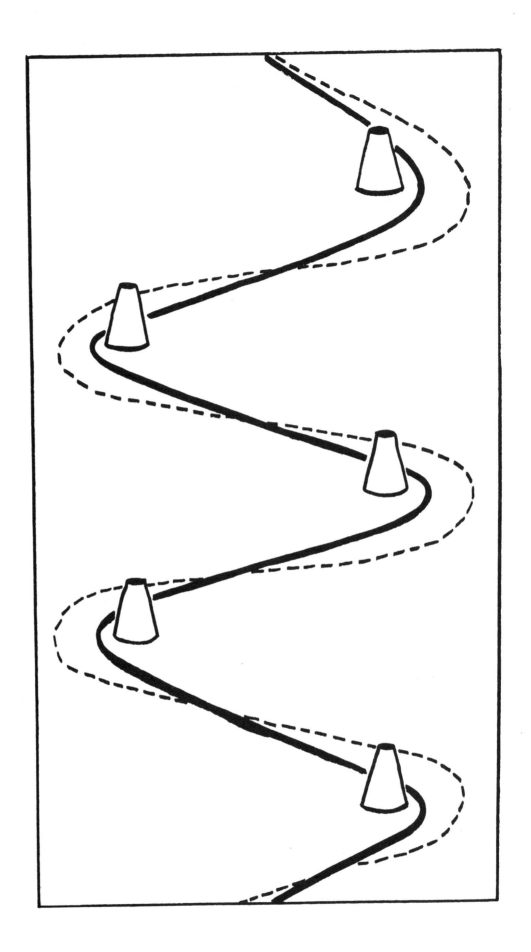

yourself, but you can crouch down and, by pointing your arms forward, you can create a foil to break the resistance. This process, called fairing (see figure 4-d), is the key to achieving the greatest speed possible with a given board on a given slope.

Conversely, to slow down, the skater must rise, thus increasing the body

4d   The air foil position reduces air resistance and thus increases speed.

surface to resistance and thereby decreasing speed. Bear in mind that at high speeds, any variation in terrain or body movement is vastly exaggerated. A bump or shift in body position that would be relatively unnoticeable at reduced speeds can literally throw your board and your body into fits at high speeds.

Empty swimming pools (see figure 4-e) attract many skaters, but they can be extremely dangerous even if you know what you're doing. Even though the speed factor in a swimming pool is considerably reduced, you're forced to contend with the possibility of losing traction at a high point of the pool and falling straight down. Because the fall is vertical and not lateral, rolling won't do you much good. Arm, wrist, and head injuries are almost a sure result of the kind of quick, straight drop experienced in a pool.

If you're really interested in this form of skating and have developed your skill fully in every other aspect of the sport, the best advice for learning is to watch someone who knows how to handle a pool situation. Essentially, what you'll see is this: the skater starts at the shallow end of the pool

Dave Abell

4e   An empty swimming pool is an attractive terrain but one that poses danger even for the most skilled skater.

4f Less radical but still very challenging terrains are drainage and flood control areas. Extended wall length and more relaxed angles provide for extended rides.

Dave Abell

facing into the bottom. Speed is developed and the skater and board climb the end wall of the pool, feet at approximately right angles to the length of the board, arms outstretched. As soon as the skater's speed begins to decrease noticeably, he or she must begin the descent, for it is the momentum that allows the skater to ride the side of the pool vertically. The instant the board breaks traction (begins to slide), the fun is over.

A short board is mandatory for pool riding in order to execute the radical curves.

Other terrains such as flood-control areas and reservoirs (see figure 4-f) are a lot of fun because you can ride the sides of the bowl without really becoming vertical. In addition, because the walls lack the steepness of a swimming pool, you can ride up and down, back and forth just about as long as you want. Again, these areas are for advanced skaters and demand proper safety equipment.

FREE-STYLE 5 TRICKS

WE'RE TOLD OF certain Indian tribes that upheld the practice of tossing the very young braves into the water as a means of teaching them to swim. Hence, the old adage "sink or swim." Whether such a teaching method had any real merit is debatable. Certainly many swam, but many also probably sank. In any event, swimming may very well be an instinctive response even for a small child. Rotating a skateboard 360 degrees on one foot, however, is not. Another old adage that is far more applicable to freestyle skating is "You can't run until you've learned to walk." In other words, don't attempt tricks that are out of the scope of your present ability.

Granted, each new trick attempted is a feat never before approached by a given skater. It's true, you'll never know if you can successfully execute a freestyle move until you try it. You can, however, have a fairly good idea. For instance, if you haven't achieved near-perfect board control during a forward ride or basic turn, you can be assured that success at any freestyle maneuver will be luck at best. Similarly, you'll never be able to perform a 360-degree spin unless you can confidently execute a kick turn.

In short, being aware of your capabilities at any time is basically a matter of common sense. Many skateboard tricks are related to each other in underlying principles of motion, balance, and strength. The following outline of freestyle tricks is presented with these categories of skills in mind. Obviously, each trick overlaps into all of the categories; my intent is to single out what I think is the most essential aspect of each. Whether you'll have more success with one group of tricks than another depends solely on your inborn ability. I would say, however, that with practice none of the tricks is too difficult for someone with reasonable strength and coordination.

When learning new tricks, make sure you are adequately protected and, again, don't push it. Some tricks will require more attention to safety-equipment precautions, but these will be obvious. Most importantly, have patience with yourself, concentrate, and skate as an individual, free from group pressure.

Body-Position Tricks

(1) Hang ten (see figure 5-a): The most rudimentary of skateboard tricks, derived from surfing, simply involves placing both feet up to the nose of the board while in motion. In terms of body control, hanging ten depends on the skater's ability to equalize his or her weight on the heels so as to prevent the rear wheels from rising off the ground. Variations include hanging five, which as the name implies involves moving one foot to the nose of the board and sitting down. To achieve this position, place your feet in the hang-ten position, squat down, place one hand at the tail of the board, and lower yourself to the desired distance from the board.

(2) Walking (see figure 5-b): Although balance is a large part of walking tricks, repositioning of the body is the essence of this maneuver. The length of your board will determine how many steps you can take. Either foot may be crossed over or behind the other in any sequence.

(3) Christie (see figure 5-c): Here, again, balance is crucial, but in its simplest form, the trick is one of body position. Pick up a comfortable amount of speed, positioning either foot in the center of the board; crouch and extend the other foot forward or to the side. Arms can be extended forward or to the sides. This move is particularly effective on turns and can be brought into a slide.

(4) Coffin (see figure 5-d): This basic position is also self-explanatory. Board control is extremely difficult here, so watch where you're heading and how fast you're getting there.

5a Hang ten

5b Walking

5c   Christie

5d   Coffin   67

5e Two-foot nose wheelie

Balance

(5) Wheelies: The principle involved in the various wheelie tricks is the positioning of one or both of your feet at one end of the board and raising the wheels on the opposite end. For all wheelies, body movement should be kept to a minimum, the knees should be slightly bent, and the arms should be extended forward, to the sides, or above your head, and a comfortable speed should be attained.

(a) Two-foot nose wheelie (see figure 5-e): Since you don't have a free leg available to equalize your weight in the two-foot nose or tail wheelie, balance must be achieved through use of the arms.

(b) One-foot nose wheelie (see figure 5-f).

(c) Two-foot tail wheelie (see figure 5-g).

(d) One-foot tail wheelie (see figure 5-h).

5f   One-foot nose wheelie   **5g**   Two-foot tail wheelie

5h   One-foot tail wheelie

5i Daffy

(6) Daffy (see figure 5-i): Basically the Daffy is a nose wheelie on the back and a tail wheelie on the front. Begin the trick on one board with another positioned a few yards ahead. While moving at a comfortable speed, stay on the nose of the riding board. As you approach the forward board, go into a one-foot nose wheelie; place your free foot on the tail of the forward board, bringing its nose up. This is a relatively easy trick once you've mastered the nose and tail wheelies.

Board Control

(7) Kick turn (see figure 5-j): This move can be performed to any angle of turn and either backside or frontside (pictured here). To gain momentum, begin by turning your upper body slightly in the opposite direction of the turn. Raise the front wheels by weighting your back foot and unweighting your front. Then rotate your upper body in the direction of the turn. Slight side-to-side kick turns can help propel you forward on flat surfaces.

(8) Endover (see figure 5-k): This trick is basically a series of nose and tail kick turns in alternating directions. Place your feet at the extreme ends of the board and rotate your body in the direction of the first kick turn.

5j   Kick turn

5k   Endover   **1**

2

3

Raise either the front or rear wheels and kick turn. Alternate kick turns, repeatedly bringing one end of the board around in front of the other.

(9) 360-degree spin: This trick can be performed in several variations: nose or tail, backside or frontside, one foot or two, or any combination of these. The maneuver is related to the kick turn but, while a kick turn brings the skater around through only a fraction of a circle, the 360-degree spin is a complete rotation.

(a) Frontside 360-degree (see figure 5-1): Your feet should be over the ends of the board as you bring your upper body back slightly in the opposite direction of the turn for momentum. Weight down with your back foot and raise the front wheels as you begin to whip your arms in the direction of the turn. Rotate your upper body completely and bring the board around in a full circle. Arms can be held forward, out to the sides, or above the head, palms facing in the pirouette position. Incidentally, the pirouette position can be applied to many tricks for added visual effect.

2

3

4

5m   Backside 360-degree   **1**

(b) Backside 360-degree (see figure 5-m): Identical to the frontside spin except the turn is executed in the opposite direction.

As mentioned, these basic maneuvers can be varied by spinning on the front wheel instead of the back, by turning in the one-foot or two-foot nose- or tail-wheelie position, or by executing multiple 360-degree turns without stepping off the board.

3

4

Body Control

(10) Power slide (see figure 5-n): You should be going between eight and fifteen miles an hour to get the right action for this trick. Lower your center of gravity as you begin your turn. Place both hands on the ground as you come around, and pivot, breaking the wheels' traction. This can also be done with a one-hand pivot. You can add other dimensions to the trick by varying the degree to which you stretch out in the slide. Sliding in a full extension (shown here), however, is somewhat more difficult.

5n   Power slide   1

2

5o   Spinner   1

2

3

(11) Spinner (see figure 5-o): At a comfortable speed, bend your knees, cocking your upper body slightly in the opposite direction of the spin. Throw your arms around and jump off the board, rotating 360-degrees in the air before landing on the board.

5p   Aerial

(12) Aerial (see figure 5-p): Sometimes called the gorilla grip, this trick is rather difficult but also rather impressive and must be executed with your shoes off. Begin the move by placing your feet on the ends of the board and curling your toes under it. Go into a crouch and leap up, bringing the board with you. This trick can be done while moving, from a standing position, or off a ramp. You can also add a 180- or 360-degree turn variation.

Strength

(13) L-Sit (see figure 5-q): Center yourself and place your hands on the ends of the board. You may either grip the board or simply rest on it as you lift yourself and extend your legs forward. Depending on your strength and degree of balance, this trick can be performed from a standing position or while moving.

5q   L-Sit

5r   V-Sit

    (14) V-Sit (see figure 5-r): Identical to the L-Sit except that the legs are brought up, forming a right or acute angle to your upper body.

(15) Handstand (see figure 5-s): Performed in the same fashion as a regular handstand. Place your hands on the ends of the board (you can also hold it), push the board off, and pick up momentum as you bring yourself into the handstand position.

5s   Handstand wheelie   **1**

2   **3**

(16) Handstand wheelie (see figure 5-t): Same as the straight handstand with addition of a nose or tail wheelie.

5t   Handstand wheelie

6 REPAIR AND MAIN-TENANCE

A COUPLE OF years ago I owned a 1962 Plymouth. Although it ran well enough and got me around with no problems, it was ugly as sin. It was so totally lacking in class and so uncomfortable to sit in that I had very little if any interest in seeing to it that the old thing was properly taken care of. One rainy morning about seven o'clock, as I was attempting to get on one of the Los Angeles freeways, the car stopped and refused to start. It had been running poorly lately, but I had never expected it to give in completely.

Well, it cost me sixty-five dollars for a major tune-up, not to mention the discomfort of being cold and wet as I waited for the mechanic to get around to fixing it. What's more, if you're familiar with L.A. freeways, you know that stalling out in the right lane as cars barrel down the road at fifty or sixty miles an hour can be very bad for your health. Despite the aggravation of the day and the money I had to get together and fork over to the mechanic, I got off pretty easy considering I could have ended up under the wheels of some semi that might not have been able to stop in time to avoid my car.

Anyway, the point of the story is simple. If I'd had more concern for the old Plymouth, awful looking as it was, that costly and potentially fatal incident would never have occurred. A routine tune-up that I could have done myself for about ten dollars would have prevented the whole mess. Although your skateboard is obviously nowhere near as complex as an automobile, the occasional repair and maintenance will enhance the board's performance, prolong its life, and keep you out of some dangerous situations. In fact, a complete skateboard tune-up will take you less than an hour and cost between nothing and a few bucks, depending on what (if anything) needs replacement.

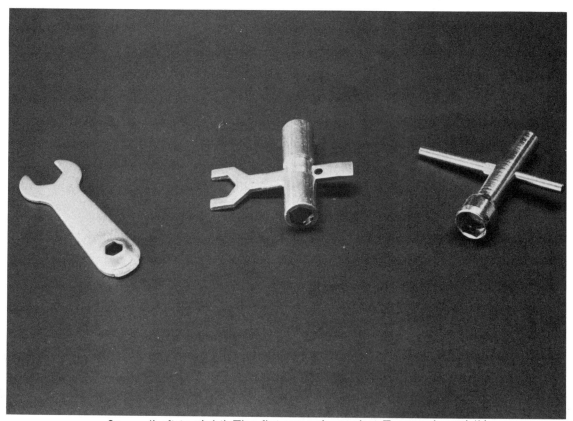

6a (Left to right) The flat wrench, socket T wrench and "4-Way Tool" are the most common skateboard repair tools. The 4-Way combines the features of the other two and costs about $3.

To completely break down and adjust the truck assembly, you shouldn't need anything more than the "four-way tool" (see figure 6-a) and a hammer. The other tools shown are also available, but the 4-Way is by far the most complete one available. It will fit the cone nuts, locknuts, action bolt, action nut, and probably your hanger plate mounting nuts as well. The screwdriver on the other end of the open-end wrench will adjust your action bolt if it's a screw head rather than a bolt head. If you buy one (the cost is about three dollars), make sure you indicate whether your axle is 5/16 or 9/32 of an inch.

First off, lay out an old towel to work on so the ball bearings won't scatter when you shake them out of the wheel.

Now, to begin the breakdown, remove the hanger plate and truck from the board; then, by loosening the action bolt and nut, remove the truck from the hanger plate. Next, take the wheels off the axle by removing the locknut, D washer, and cone nut. As I said, when you do this, be careful the bearings don't scatter. Finally, unscrew the action nut and pull the bolt through the cushions. Go about this one truck at a time so you don't inundate yourself with washers, nuts, and whatnot.

6b

When you get the whole thing taken apart (see figure 6-b), you're ready to begin inspection, cleaning, and replacement of worn parts. First, you'll want to clean the ball bearings. You only have to roll them around in a tissue or rag, but do each one separately. Lubricating the bearings is not advisable, in my opinion, for the simple reason that lubricants are sticky and readily attract dirt. To my knowledge, no truly dry lubricant is currently on the market. If and when a dry one is available, you might want to give it a try. If the bearings are really gooped up, clean them with a little gasoline or similar solvent, but make sure they're fully dried to prevent rusting. Do the same for all nuts and washers. Cleaning these parts is a precaution against particle buildup, which can freeze them and make on-the-spot tune-ups a real hassle.

Also clean the wheels' races by covering your finger with a rag and rubbing it around the race. You may want to substitute a screwdriver for your

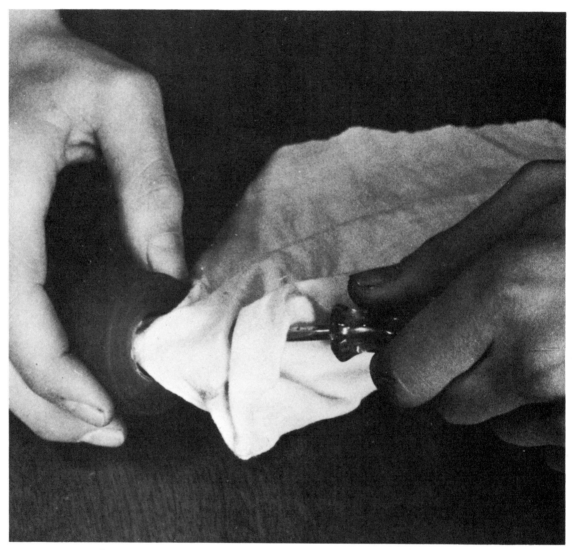

6c

finger if the race is heavily laden with caked dirt (see figure 6-c). If you must use a solvent to remove grease and gunk, do so very carefully, so as to stay clear of the urethane part of the wheel. Solvents will attack the plastic and can deform the wheel substantially if enough is applied.

The next step is to clean the axle threads. Again, this will prevent dirt buildup, which can freeze the cone and locknuts. If there's any question in your mind as to whether your axle is bent, take it out and inspect it. You can remove it by tapping one end with a hammer. The axle has lateral lines at a point just off the center which hold it in the housing. If it doesn't come out after tapping one end, try the other: there's no way to tell which way it will come out. Once loosened in this manner, simply pull the axle out, look straight down the length of it, and roll it on a flat surface. If it's bent, don't go any farther. This could pose serious problems and you should buy another (cost is between fifty cents and $1.50, depending on length and manufacturer). If your axle is straight, clean and replace it the same way you took it out.

At this point, you'll also want to inspect the cushions. If you've been detecting some problem with them, or if they appear radically deformed replace them too. These will run about twenty-five cents apiece. While you're at it, check the retainer caps and replace them if they're at all bent. The cushions should sit flatly in the caps and, if they're bent, it could affect the overall action of the truck. Retainer caps are also about twenty-five cents apiece.

The action bolt should wear pretty well, but if for some reason it's been bent or threads have been stripped, get another. The price of a new one will be no more than fifty cents. Also check the pivot bushing (no more than thirty cents apiece) for wear. If you keep the pivot point and socket clean, wear to this area should also be minimal.

Before you begin to remount the wheels, check them for wear. Hard skating, high speeds, and radical turning will wear the wheels down. Even though urethane is very tough stuff, it, like all materials used in skateboard parts, will deteriorate with time. If the wheels are worn on the outside, it's probably due to riding habits. Rotating the wheels (putting the right front on the left rear, left front on the right rear, etc.) with each breakdown will slow this normal wearing process. If, however, you detect excessive wear on the inside of the wheel, chances are you've got a bent axle. Even if you've already checked the axle for straightness, do so again when this wear situation is present.

Now you're ready to replace the ball bearings and wheels. Put the wheel back on the axle and replace the cone nut, D washer, and locknut. These should be tightened down just slightly. Now, hold the truck so the wheel is resting on your working surface (see figure 6-d). Hold the wheel down, pull the truck up by the pivot arm, and drop inside bearings in one at a time (they shouldn't be bunched up between the race and cone nut); let the truck down and spin it (still holding the wheel down) to make sure the bearings are properly seated.

When the inside bearings are seated, pull the wheel in to the truck and pick the assembly up so you can seat the outside bearings (see figure 6-e). Drop the bearings in and tighten the cone nut down so that the wheel's spin is visibly impaired. Then bring the cone nut back up slowly until you reach the optimum spinning point. There will be some wobble at this point,

6d

6e

but it should be very slight. When the desired spin is achieved, tighten the locknut down, holding the cone nut in place. Repeat this procedure for all wheels. Ideally, all four wheels should spin at the same rate.

If your wheels are of the self-contained variety, the process is slightly different and a little simpler because there's no cone adjustment necessary. To get the bearings out of the wheel, slip a screwdriver into the bearing housing and apply pressure to the small groove on the shaft of the male

6f

section. Clean the bearings, races, and bearing housing as you would for a loose-ball wheel. Replace the bearings by inserting the male section into the wheel and dropping the balls into the race (see figure 6-f). Now, turn the wheel over and place it on a stack of quarters or some hard cylindrical object. This will serve as a support block when you hammer the male section into the female.

Holding your finger on the opening in the male section, drop in the remaining bearings (see figure 6-g). When all the bearings have been replaced, set the female section in the center of the wheels and tap it in with a hammer until the two parts are locked (see figure 6-h).

6g

6h

6i

6j

Once the wheels are mounted, run the action bolt through the top retainer cap and bushing and through the lower bushing and retainer cap so that the cushions are seated flatly. Replace the action nut so that only a few threads of the action bolt are visible. First insert the bolt into the socket and then the pivot arm into the pivot socket (see figure 6-i). Now, holding the action nut with your fingers or another wrench, tighten down the action bolt (see figure 6-j). At this point, you're on your own because determining truck action (which is adjusted by tightening the action bolt) is strictly personal. The only guideline here is that a loose truck will give you a more mobile board, while a tight truck is imperative for high-speed skating to reduce board wobble. When you get the desired action (you'll probably want to wait until the truck is mounted on the board to determine this), tighten the action nut down to the socket in which the action bolt is inserted.

Lastly, replace shock or elevator pads if you have them and mount the truck to the board (see figure 6-k).

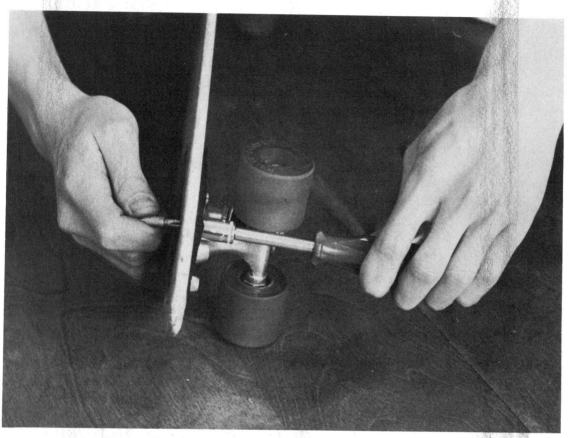

6k

You're probably wondering how often you should go about this process. I wish I had a prescription; frequency of upkeep, however, is determined by the amount and kind of skating you do and the type of terrain you ride on. Being aware of the condition of your equipment is the best way to keep it running well. If the truck looks dirty, if you hear grit rubbing in the bearings, or if the wheel spin is noticeably impaired, you'll want to break it down and clean it. Of course, should you lose a bearing in the course of riding, you'll have to replace it without waiting too long. One missing bearing, although it might not immediately affect your ride, will cause some side-to-side play in the board and will eventually knock out the rest of the bearings. Anytime you have to replace a bearing, you might as well clean and tune the whole truck, as you'll have to take time to break down one wheel anyway.

As mentioned earlier, precision bearings require little or no maintenance. In fact, because the bearings are sealed, or at least partially shielded, there really isn't a whole lot you can do in terms of cleaning the unit. Wear and dirt accumulation should be minimal, but if the bearings do begin to get gunked up, pop the unit out and replace it. They usually run about $1.25 apiece. If you break the seal on a precision bearing, you'll never be able to replace it securely enough to insulate the bearings against dirt buildup. And because precision bearings are packed in a rather heavy lubricant, such buildup will be immediate and severe.

Another thing to remember about precision bearings is that they're not compatible with loose-ball wheels. Don't try to put a precision unit in a wheel designed for loose ball bearings. Because the loose-ball wheel is molded to hold the race, you'll never be able to adequately install a precision bearing, which requires a flat seat. On top of that, tightening down of the locknut will put pressure on the precision unit, which in turn puts pressure on the hollowed-out seat for the race. The result will be deformation of the urethane. If, by some luck, you were able to properly seat the precision unit in the first place, pressure from the locknut and deformation of the urethane would quickly unalign the precision housing.

Should you incur dents on a fiberglass, wood, or aluminum board, you'll want to sand these down. Splinters from any of these materials will be almost unavoidable if you ride without shoes. Start with a coarse-grade sandpaper and bring the dent to the desired level. Once you've done this, take a finer grade finishing paper and smooth the area out.

If you get a board that's not predrilled for truck mounting, you'll want to use a #8 wood screw, about ⅝ of an inch in length for a plastic or wood board. For all other materials, use an 8-32 flat-headed machine screw. Mount the front truck so that there is a distance of about 2½ to 4 inches between the nose of the board and the front of the hanger plate; with the back truck, there should be about three to five inches from the tail to the back of the hanger plate. These figures are based on a twenty-seven-inch board, which is about average. The shorter the distance between the trucks, the more radical the turning radius but also the less stability overall.

COMPE-
7 TITION
SKATING

ANY SPORT CAN be enjoyed in some form outside the framework of a formal competition. Skateboarding lends itself very well to noncompetitive activity, but the fact that human beings seem to thrive on matching skills against one another applies here as well. Competition skating is neither desirable nor undesirable in any absolute way. It's strictly up to the individual. There are plenty of outstanding skaters who have never competed, but those who do compete successfully gain not only recognition but self-esteem, a feeling all of us strive for in one way or another.

Unfortunately, competition skating is by no means widespread; the opportunities it affords are therefore not available to everyone. Skating competitions were held as far back as 1965 in southern California, but for the moment the rebirth of these events has remained confined to this area. Lately southern California has experienced no shortage of skating competitions and, from the looks of things, this trend will be spreading across the country. As organizations expand and individuals begin to get together, competition events will probably reach even the Midwest, which appears to be the least developed area in terms of skateboard enthusiasm. The proof

7a Chris Yandall executes a one-foot nose wheelie at the
Orange County Fairgrounds in Southern California.

Warren Bolster (Courtesy of Skateboarder Magazine)

is in the number of requests received by skateboard organizations in southern California for information on how to set up a competition.

In order to give some idea of where this aspect of skating is currently and where it's going, I'll run down the competition situation as it's developing in southern California.

As it stands right now, there are really two categories of competition. First there are those sanctioned by either of the two primary skateboard organizations: the Pro/Am Skateboard Racers Association and the United States Skateboard Association. Sanctioning basically means that the organization involved sets up and oversees the competition, keeps records, and officially recognizes it as a legitimate event, much the way other athletic organizations do for various sports. But the events take money, so sponsors are needed. Often a manufacturer will fund the competition and attach its name to it. From the sponsor's point of view, backing the event financially means good publicity.

The second broad type of competition is that which is approved rather than sanctioned. In this category are those held by a city's parks and recreation department (which has land and manpower resources), chambers of commerce, or other noncommercial groups. What differentiates this type from a sanctioned event is money. Because the sponsoring group can't afford the full services of an organization, they receive only consultation. The organization's approval comes once they are reasonably sure (because they have laid the groundwork for the event) it will come up to their standards. Because they don't actually have a direct hand in the competition and will not be overseeing it, they reserve their sanction. It's the organization's safeguard in case their advice either goes awry or simply isn't heeded.

Once the initial business is taken care of, concrete plans for the event are laid out. The role of the sanctioning group then is to provide expertise so that the event is fairly and efficiently run. Location, judging standards and judges, type of events held, number of entrants allowed, fees, etc., are all carefully mapped out. But don't get the impression that things always run smoothly. On the contrary, plenty of competitions have been botched beyond belief. But, as things become more standardized, as the people involved fail and succeed and learn, competitions improve.

Numerous variables come into play once the site is selected. First, the organizers must determine whether the competition will be a one-day event or whether it will extend, say, over a weekend. Because as many as 350 skaters have entered some competitions, two-day events generally work out best, with the first day being devoted to qualification events and the second to finals.

The next thing to consider is exactly which events will comprise the competition. Always included are a freestyle event and slalom run, but speed skating is more often than not disregarded in competition. A banked freestyle event is being included more and more frequently, but, as of the moment, it hasn't come into its own.

Who will compete against whom? This question can be answered in a variety of ways, but most often the entrants are first broken down into groups by sex and then by age. Age can also be handled in a variety of ways. Each sex group can be roughly divided into a junior and a senior class or into more specific groupings. The SRA prefers three classes in both female and male categories: ages ten to twelve, thirteen to sixteen, and seventeen and over.

Entrance qualifications have been pretty lax so far, but both major skateboard organizations have expressed a desire to make membership in their group mandatory. As the organizations build their point rating system, this requirement, as well as point requirements for national or regional events, will make sense. Also, an entry fee of anywhere from fifty cents to three dollars is usually required.

7b   Bruce Logan goes for a headstand spinner at the Bahne-Cadillac National Skateboard Championships at the Del Mar Fairgrounds, Del Mar, Calif.   *Warren Bolster (Courtesy of Skateboarder Magazine)*

Specific guidelines for the events involved must also be spelled out. As mentioned, competition is still in its very early stages, so standard rules have yet to be recognized universally. A hypothetical situation will give you some idea, though, of what can be expected. Focusing on freestyle, two events must be held in each classification—an elimination and a final competition. In the preliminary event, each skater will be allowed 1½ minutes to perform on a maximum of two boards, while the finals will entail two-minute performances. Each of the events will be conducted in an area fifty feet square with a brief warm-up period provided in advance for all skaters. No props will be allowed other than the ramps (which we'll provide for this example) and a high-jump bar.

Each skater will be evaluated by three judges on the basis of the number of tricks performed, the continuity or flow of the performance, control of the board, and overall style. Points will be given on a scale of one to ten, including half-points. Evaluation will not be based on the degree of difficulty of the tricks. Since new tricks are always being incorporated into freestyle routines, this would be impossible.

While judges may not necessarily have specific expertise in skateboarding, they will be selected on the basis of their knowledge of dance, gymnastics, surfing, or skiing. As the sport progresses, skaters will be able to judge competitions, but right now, those skaters involved in competition are competing. For a major event, seven judges would be ideal, with the high and low scores being thrown out.

To overcome the common problem of judges coming and going (being replaced by other individuals who may have different standards of evaluation), the three judges in our example will have to judge all entrants in the freestyle event.

Five semifinalists will be chosen in the preliminary event; these five will then compete in the final event. Only the top three in the finals will place.

Now let's move on to the slalom event. Fortunately we've got a natural hill, so we won't have to mess around with an artificial ramp. The run will total about 110 yards with the last ten being flat ground. The hill slopes at about a twenty-five-degree angle and curves about midway. Cones will be arranged in a switchback configuration about six feet apart. Because of the curve in the road, only one skater will run at a time, as the outside rider on a two-man course would be at an obvious disadvantage. Electronic timing lights will be used, as in snow skiing, to eliminate any inaccuracy that might result from a stopwatch.

If the skater falls or steps the board, he or she will be disqualified, but knocking over a cone, as long as the skater goes around it, will only result in a 1/10 of a second penalty.

7c   Barrel jumping is ordinarily not included as a competition event but rather a kind of half-time novelty.   *Dave Abell*

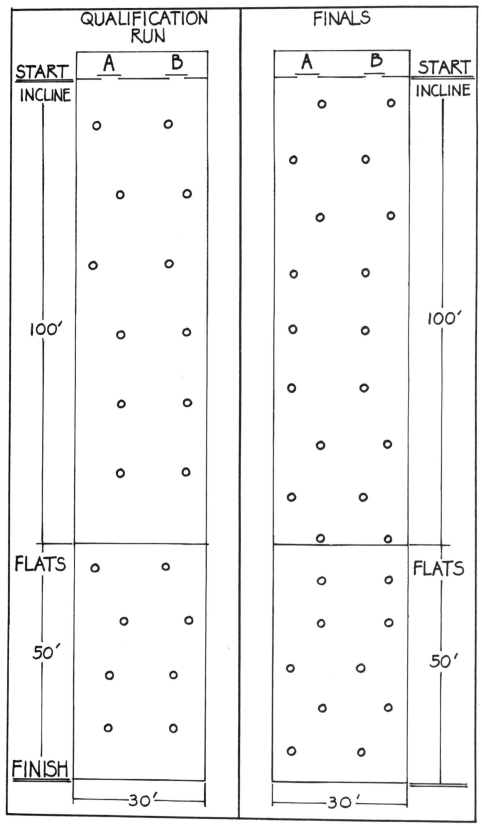

7d The slalom ramp constructed for the Bahne-Cadillac Championships.

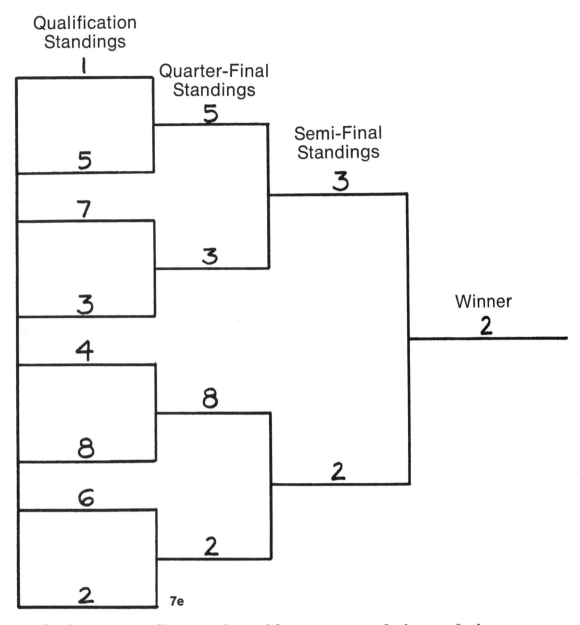

Qualification Standings
1
5
7
3
4
8
6
2

Quarter-Final Standings
5
3
8
2

Semi-Final Standings
3
2

Winner
2

7e

The slalom event will consist of a qualification, a quarterfinal, a semifinal, and a final run. The top eight skaters in the qualification will compete against each other in the quarterfinals, eliminating four. The remaining four will then compete in the semifinals, eliminating two. The final run will determine the winner of the event (see figure 7-e). Since our competition will be held over two days, the qualification and quarterfinals will be held the first day and the semifinals and finals the second.

(After the qualification run, it would be possible to allow each skater two runs, taking the best as the determining time.)

As in all slalom events, wearing a helmet will be mandatory.

This outline is a very simplistic view of competition. On top of additional specifics that vary with each contest, there's an amazing amount of business

7f

and supervision to be attended to. Skateboard organizations are just beginning to scratch the surface of competition potential, but the energy and certainly the interest are there. It's just going to take a lot of effort, primarily on the part of the skateboard organizations, but also on the part of every skater who has an interest in developing the sport through formal competition.

SKATE-
8 BOARD
ORGANI-
ZATIONS

SKATEBOARDING WILL CONTINUE to grow if for no other reason than that it's fun. But it's going to take a lot of work in terms of personal and group effort to transform skating into a recognized sport. Any new activity, idea, or product must go through this period of acceptance.

Individual enthusiasm can promote skateboarding through word of mouth, but massive organization is needed to consolidate interests, coordinate competitions, promote product innovations, and rally public support and assistance.

Four major skateboard organizations exist at present for just this reason. All of the groups have similar goals and need participation to see them through. I'm not advocating membership in any of the organizations in a blanket way. You may be content to take your board to a favorite spot and skate away alone or with a group of friends. And this is fine. But if you're interested in furthering the goal of establishing skateboarding as a sport, or if you'd just like to be kept informed and share in a group experience, membership in skateboard organizations may suit you.

Again, the problem is that all of these organizations are focused in southern California. Growth, however, can only come about as group officials see interest developing in other parts of the country. This means membership. If you're looking to walk into a fully developed organization, forget it. These groups are more in the embryonic stage than in infancy. But if you care to invest in the future of the sport, to get in at the beginning, check out the alternatives. Somebody's got to start the ball rolling, and if you're interested, you might as well be one of the initiators.

The following is a list of the organizations and a brief statement about each. I would strongly suggest, however, that you send for information before making a membership commitment. My remarks will give you some idea of what's available, but they should only serve to point you in the right direction.

(1) Pro/Am Skateboard Racers Association (SRA): Parent company is Sports Market Production, Inc. SRA organizes, sanctions, and approves competitions, seeking to establish the sport through such events. It is also attempting to design and construct skateboard parks. SRA is currently working with the Los Angeles Parks and Recreation Department to set up a citywide competition, and with manufacturers to promote production and use of safety equipment. The organization has established regional representation in Japan and is seeking the same throughout the United States.

Membership (open to anyone) is four dollars and includes an SRA patch, decal, and periodical newsletter. Membership will also qualify you for participation in SRA-sanctioned competitions and point ranking system. SRA also has plans to provide insurance for members who skate in SRA parks at such time as these facilities are constructed.

Contact: SRA
33159 Camino Capistrano, Suite B
San Juan Capistrano, California 97675
(714) 493-9851

(2) United States Skateboard Association (USSA): Nonprofit organization set up to establish safety standards, competition, judging formats, and rider classification system. This system involves ranking from A to AAAA classes accumulated in USSA-sanctioned competition. USSA plans to work with local governments to search out, develop, and preserve skating sites.

Membership costs one dollar and is open to anyone, regardless of geographical area. With membership you'll get a USSA sticker and will become qualified to participate in USSA-sanctioned competitions.

Contact: USSA
2236 Pacific Avenue
San Pedro, California 90731
(213) 547-1588

(I should add that it can be pretty hard to contact representatives of the USSA.)

(3) California Skateboard Association (CSA): Established to promote safety, skill, and sportsmanship. CSA provides information to members on aspects of the sport and laws regulating it.

Membership is restricted to California residents and costs one dollar. Patch, decal, and newsletter are provided with membership. For a ten-dollar membership fee, the CSA will provide a medical insurance policy.

(4) International Professional Skateboard Association (IPSA): Affiliated with the CSA, the IPSA accredits teachers who instruct CSA members in various facets of skateboarding, including skills, techniques, body conditioning, safety, and business aspects of the sport. It also provides local governments and government agencies with information on skateboarding.

9 FROM DRAINAGE BASINS TO CEMENT WAVES

EARLY IN 1976, when I was getting together the first edition of *The Skateboard Book*, skaters all over Southern California were beginning to talk longingly of the future of skateboarding in terms of skateboard parks. It wasn't hard to understand why. Although the sport was truly only in its formative stages, many skaters were already pushing the limits of flat ground and sloped freestyle. Skaters (many of them not yet ready to make the transition) were flocking to places like drainage basins to take advantage of relatively suitable vertical surfaces.

But these spots—even the favorites—were not always the best. Obviously, they had been designed for purposes quite different than skateboarding, and the concrete was often coarse and occasionally cracked. In addition, transitions (the gradient angle or curve from flat to vertical) were often nearly unridable. Unfortunately, the only way to discover that was by trial and error, and believe me, the error part of the process was in many cases severe.

What's more, trespassing in these areas was illegal. Not infrequently, skaters were driven from city-owned drainage facilities by hovering helicopters, only to be met down the road by a patrolman or two, waiting with a few choice words and summonses. Eventually, "preventive action" was taken by cities. "Killer bumps" and railroad ties were laid, transforming basins into death-defying obstacle courses.

The response by skaters was sometimes fierce. Nightraids on basins found groups of irate skaters hacking at the obstacles with pick axes and sledge hammers.

Throughout this mess of action-counteraction, skaters were suffering legal and physical repercussions. Juvenile courts and hospital emergency wards were hopping. The branching out of the sport had expanded problems from street accidents and pedestrian-traffic hassles. More than ever, in the ensuing year, skaters, city officials and others found themselves searching for an answer to the injuries, the legal skirmishes, and the general inconvenience.

At the time, there seemed to be some salvation in city park and recreation departments. They were the logical answer to increasing problems. After all, it's their duty to provide adequate recreation facilities. Slowly, they seemed to be responding. Ventura, Ca., opened a rather tame skateboard track and it looked like other cities might start following suit. Organized community pressure on city governments could have provided the answer.

But never underestimate the power of free enterprise or overestimate the capabilities of the average city. Obviously much more was involved than laying concrete in an available space. Less obvious was the ability of cities to bring design to a more sophisticated level and to provide necessary supervision.

A move was already afoot in Southern California to develop the skate-park concept and turn it into an effective and, yes, money-making proposition. The process had begun in 1974 actually. Lou Peralta, an entertainer, film-maker and entrepreneur, had approached the City of Los Angeles with the idea for a skatepark. Drawing on his knowledge of moto-cross and skateboarding, Peralta had designed a unique continuous course with banked walls up to 13-feet high. It had never been done before and as Peralta recalls, "Nobody told me not to do it; in fact the city was receptive to the idea—but nobody was ready to stand completely behind me."

His justification for the park was based on the fact that all sports have some form of arena for participation, but skateboarding was still floundering as a renegade activity. There were millions of skaters but no place to

9a Establishing the Ventura Skateboard Park in Ventura, Calif. took a co-operative community effort. Rather tame, it's a good spot for learning and casual skating.

9b Photo by Stan Sharp

skate in complete safety. Peralta met with various city officials; he undertook environmental impact studies, traffic reports, and insurance reports. His goal was to educate the city and, in so doing, pave the way for others.

Some months later, with Peralta still bogged down in red tape, John O'Malley, a forerunner in skateboard organization, came up with the idea for the Carlsbad, Ca., skatepark. By the time Peralta obtained a preliminary building permit two years later, Carlsbad was already under construction.

Finally, Peralta's Skatercross in Reseda, Ca., became a reality. Superior Gunite was contracted to lay down the shotcrete (a pneumatically applied form of concrete) and Peralta was in business.

Soon the Concrete Wave in Anaheim, Ca., opened, as well as parks in San Diego, El Cajon, and Montebello, Ca. Wild tales of a skatepark bonanza began to make the rounds. Entrepreneurs were lured by claims that $70,000 could be made in the first month of operation. Seminars were conducted for prospective builders, design plans were sold, and the rush to build bigger and better was on.

But the "skatepark boom" was still a disorganized, every-man-for-himself proposition. The simple fact is, there was a lot of ripping-off going on in terms of building, financing, designing, and insuring. All the while, Peralta looked on at construction prices pushing $500,000 and skyrocketing insurance rates. Unity was needed.

Peralta made the move to open the lines of communication among skatepark owners. A meeting was arranged with O'Malley and representatives from the Concrete Wave and a few other parks. A month later, the Association of Skatepark Owners, Inc. was formed. Insurance, safety, operational procedures, equipment and school programs, and competition became the orders of business.

Development in the meantime was phenomenal, with parks opening throughout the country. One of them was the Endless Wave in Bakersfield, Ca., constructed by Superior Gunite under the watchful eyes of Gary Doane and Ed Olson. Superior had reportedly constructed about 75% of the parks in Southern California and was developing a growing awareness that park design required heavier emphasis on actual participation of knowledgeable skaters. When Doane and Olson went to Oxnard, Ca., to create The Endless Wave II, they relied to a great extent on two such individuals —Jerry Valdez and Marc Smith. As Doane remarked, "We went so far as to get in there with Jerry and Marc with shovels and work and rework some of the runs and bowls ourselves."

The result is what has been referred to as "a true skater's park" and a solid move toward designing parks with sharp attention to the demands of the sport.

Design and Construction

Just what constitutes a "good park" is a rather complex matter. The most general factor is size. The Endless Wave encompasses some 30,000 sq. feet of skating surface, and is, as I mentioned, considered to be a superlative park. The range extends toward the 200,000 sq. foot mark. But the real test here is how the runs are clustered, the ratio of area allotted to the more popular runs and the number of skaters present at any given time.

As for the variety of features, this is where massive design competition is happening. Some designers believe we are rapidly approaching the point of diminishing returns where design and variety exceed the limits of the sport. Be that as it may, there seems to be a general focusing around certain features, with variation occurring within these basic boundaries. A well-

9c   World Champion Stacy Peralta (no relation to Lou Peralta) executes a kick turn on a 13-foot wall at Lou Peralta's Skatercross in Reseda, Ca.

designed park will include features that cater to different levels of ability with heavy emphasis on the most popular runs. Briefly, in ascending order of difficulty, this is what you can expect to find in terms of features:

Freestyle Area—Less and less space is being devoted to this feature as the general level of skating skill is increasing. 80 × 40 feet is a fairly standard size. The area may include slightly banked walls.

Slalom Run—Usually about 100 feet long and dropping perhaps 10 or 15 feet with small banked walls.

Snake Run—A curved channel with walls in the area of 8–12 feet high, sometimes emptying into a bowl. Moguls, variably spaced humps (as found on skiing slopes), can also be incorporated.

Pools and Bowls—These are the major attractions at most parks. Some earlier designs didn't include them, but builders in the know are adding pools and bowls if their original plans didn't include them. Depth varies from about 7 feet to between 9 and 12 feet for advanced skaters. Pools may include (and there should be at least one in a park) a slight overhanging lip around the edge.

Half-Pipes—Literally a half-pipe with no flat spot. Length and diameter are variable, 22 feet in diameter being a sufficient challenge for just about everyone. Some half-pipes go slightly beyond vertical.

Full-Pipe—Again, literally a full-pipe, completely symmetrical with no flat spot. High degree of difficulty here; high degree of thrill in getting past vertical. You won't find many, but they're on the rise, to be sure.

Of the more subtle design elements, transition is the most critical and perhaps the least understood. Measured as a radius, transition is the gradient or arc from the bottom of a sloped wall to the top. Transition dictates skateability and while most skaters are not familiar with the principle, they know when it's not right. More than a few parks have been shunned because bowl and snake run transitions were designed without regard for the dynamics of skating.

Surfaces, of course, should be, and most often are, smooth and devoid of bumps or substantial cracks, while providing adequate traction. Shotcrete is the material of choice for these reasons. Unlike swimming pools, which are fabricated from gunite, skatepark features require the structural strength provided by shotcrete. Whereas swimming pools utilize the weight of the water in them to prevent ground moisture under the structure from pushing the pool up and out of the ground, skatepark features must stand on their own. Shotcrete also is much smoother than gunite and doesn't require the plastering over typical of swimming pools.

Other surfaces are being tried. As an afterthought, several parks have added plywood ramps and half-pipes. If properly constructed, these are adequate in terms of stability and traction.

A more recent development is the molded fiberglass pre-fabricated park. Marketed by International Sports and Recreation Inc., these parks include a variety of features (most notably full-pipes). Construction and materials appear to be sound and the design seems popular enough.

The Action

On a warm Saturday afternoon at a popular skatepark, you will no doubt bear witness to skating action that is beyond dramatic and sometimes seemingly beyond human ability. To a new skater, there can be no sight more mind-blowing than the gravity-defying aerial tricks that are at last safe, thanks to appropriate park design and required safety equipment.

As with other aspects of skating skill, park skating is a matter of practice and progress. It is a fool, who after a month of skating, attempts aerial tricks; for he or she will quickly part company with his or her board and probably his or her pride.

Pride and dignity play a large role in skating, as well as in all other sports. No one wants to perform poorly, no one wants to be a beginner. It's a double bind in a way; a beginner doesn't want to go for the rudimentary activities first for fear of being labeled a novice. On the other hand, no one wants to look bad by doing something that is beyond his or her immediate scope of ability. I've mentioned that before, but I can't stress it sufficiently. Now more than ever, with the greater challenges presented by skateparks, it is an important thing to consider. Although sport is by nature always a matter of going one step beyond the tried and true, it is also a matter of knowing just how far is reasonable.

9d   A long shot of the Endless Wave in Oxnard, Ca. In the foreground, the curving snake run. On the right, the basin— ideal for beginning banked maneuvers. In the background, the unique "dual pools."

9e   Mickey McDowell works out on the plywood half-pipe
at the Paved Wave in Ocean, N.J.   *Howard Slater*

Take this basic observation to heart—no one really cares that you're not an accomplished skater. Every skater knows that you have to start somewhere. You won't be put down because you choose to begin the evolution of your skills on a slalom ramp rather than by doing three-wheelers in a bowl. Believe it or not, no one will notice. On the contrary, it is the accomplished skaters who are watched and labeled. Do what feels natural and right and then move on to some of these areas that involve vertical walls and "air."

Kick Turn, backside—(see figure 9c) Essentially that is the same trick described in the Freestyle section except that it is performed on a vertical surface. Backside means your back will be facing out (you'll be looking down). You can grab the nose of the board for added stability. This is a good beginning maneuver and can be performed first on a moderate wall in a freestyle area or snake run. The front side variation is significantly more difficult.

Three-Wheeler—(see figure 9g) This variation can be performed off a kick turn. It is simply a matter of making the turn on one wheel, with three wheels in air.

Tail Tap—(see figure 9h) Basically this is a kick turn on the tail of the board, four wheels out (in air). It's most often performed frontside, but backside is possible.

Lip Slide—Performed in a pool, move vertically up the wall, bring the board out of the pool, kick turn 180° on the rear wheels and re-enter.

Carve or Axle-Grinder—The trick is to move vertically up the wall, turning at the top and sliding the board along the coping on the trucks (hence the name Axle-Grinder). The most popular variation is front side because it looks best.

Aerial—The variety of aerial tricks is almost limitless. Aerial stunts—getting air—have one major ingredient in common, of course—all four wheels must leave the surface. Usually performed in bowls, the maneuver requires sufficient speed to bring the board up the wall and out. Obviously, you have to grip the board as you lift up. There are, however, stirrups that can be mounted on the board's surface into which you can slip your feet, thus freeing the hands. Re-entry on aerial tricks is essential. To lift your board out into thin air and extend over a 10-foot deep bowl is a feat, but if you can't re-enter smoothly on your board, it's like returning a kickoff 80 yards and getting tackled on the goal line.

Fakey—This trick is performed in a bowl and entails bringing the board up a wall and back down on the same line. It may seem simple but it is rather difficult and requires a lot of knee action. A 360° variation is possible.

Rules and Regulations

The conditions for entering (and remaining in) skateparks vary to some extent from facility to facility. Some general statements, however, can be

9f The backside kick turn is an essential preliminary to advanced park skating.

made. First of all, there's the fee, of course. This can be based on one of three plans. There's a simple hourly rate, usually in the area of $1.50. There are also session rates. This is the most frequently used plan and is modeled after ice skating rink sessions. The session is two hours and the rate is from $2.50–$3.50 per session (usually closer to the $3.00 mark). This cost may include a 25¢ insurance fee that provides complete coverage for the skater in the event of an accident. The other plan is the floating session. This involves punching a time clock and paying per minute upon leaving the park.

Initially, you will probably have to purchase an ID card from the park at a cost of about $3.00. The card must be presented each time you enter the park. It serves a few purposes. First of all, it's a way of monitoring who's in the park at any given time; in other words, it's a way of keeping track of things and simplifying supervision. Skaters who abuse privileges and violate rules will usually have their cards revoked, thus preventing them from returning and helping to keep the park free of trouble-makers (of which there seem to be very few at most parks). The card also serves as a deposit on safety equipment that you may have to rent from the park.

This is an extremely important and universal rule at skateparks: certain safety precautions must be taken by each skater. You must use the following equipment: gloves, knee pads, elbow pads and helmet. If you don't own these items, the park will rent them for 25¢ each. By the time you're fully outfitted, you may be wearing up to $16 worth of park-owned safety equipment. It should be obvious why the ID card is retained for deposit by the ownership.

9g   Jack Waterman gets three wheels out in the Endless Wave's half-pipe.

9h Jay Adams executes a picture-perfect tail tap in a 12-foot bowl at Skatercross.

9i Cutting the oping with an axle-grinding carve.

Upon entry, you will also have to sign a "liability release agreement." The form will call for your name, birthdate, place of residence and other vital information. It will also lay out the rules of the park. The remainder of the agreement can be a complicated series of conditions spelled out in complex legalese. Basically what it all adds up to is your releasing the park from any liability with respect to injury incurred on park property. In other words, upon signing the agreement, you waive your right to sue the park.

As any lawyer will tell you, the validity of the contract when signed by a minor is questionable. For this reason, many parks require a parent's signature and on top of that carry catastrophic insurance as a safeguard in case the park is sued for a very major accident. To my knowledge, such a suit has never been brought against any park. The reason is simply that, given the safety regulations, the equipment and the supervision, it's highly unlikely that a catastrophe would occur.

Finally, by signing the agreement, you grant the management of the park (or anyone else they so permit) to photograph you while you're skating. In that sense, the agreement also serves as a model release.

INDEX

A

Accidents, 11-12, 15, 20, 47, 48, 49, 58, 61
Aerial, 79
Air-foil position, 55
Air resistance, reducing, 58, 61

B

Bahne, Bob, 19
Balance, 68-70
Ball bearings, 43
Basic position, 53, 55
Benefits, skateboarding, 20-21
Board control, 70-75
Boards, 20, 22
   buying hints, 23-35

fiberglass, 19, 27-29
   safety practices and, 47
Body control, 76-77
Body-position tricks, 65
Buying, hints about, 22-43

C

Cadillac Wheels, 19
California Medical Association, 5
California Skateboard Association, 105
Campbell, Jeff, 50
Chicago Roller Skate Company, 14
Christie, 65
Coffin, 65
Competition skating, 94-102
Components, buying, 22-43

Cost of skateboards, 21
Creative Urethanes, Inc., 19

D

Daffy, 70
Downhill speed racing, 58

E

Endover, 70
Equipment
    buying hints, 22-43
    impact, 48
    safety, 47-48, 58, 62

F

Fad, skateboarding as a, 15, 19
Fairing, 61
Falling, 44, 50-52
Feet, 57
"Four-way tool," 84
Freestyle skating, 64-82

G

Gorilla grip, 79

H

Handstand, 81
Handstand wheelie, 82
Hang ten, 65
Helmets, 47-48
History, skateboarding, 13-21

I

Impact, reduction of, 50-52
Impact equipment, 48
International Professional Skateboard
    Association, 105

K

Kick turn, 70

L

Learning to skateboard, 53-57
L-Sit,79

M

Maintenance, 83-93

N

Nasworthy, Frank, 19
Nose wheelies, 68

O

Opposition to skateboarding, 11, 15, 50
Organizations, skateboard, 102, 103-
    105

P

Parallel stance, 55
Parks, skateboard, 19, 45-46
Position, basic, 53, 55
Power slide, 76
Pro/Am Skateboard Racers Associa-
    tion, 96, 104

R

Repairs, 83-93
Richards, Mark, 15

S

Safety equipment, 47-48, 58, 62
Safety practices, 44-52
Schufeldt, Denis, 49
Skateboard parks, 106

Slalom, 57-58
Speed, skateboards and, 21, 58-62
Speed skating, 58
Spinner, 77
Sport, skateboarding as a, 11-12, 14, 15, 18, 19, 20, 49
Sports Market Production, Inc., 104
Strength, 79
Swimming pools, empty, skateboarding in, 61, 62

———————

T

Tail wheelies, 68
360-degree spin, 72-75
Tricks
    body-position, 65
    freestyle, 64-82
    wheelie, 68-70
Trucks, skateboard, 14, 17, 20, 22, 35-38, 57

Turning, 57

———————

U

United States Skateboard Association, 96, 104

———————

V

Val Surf, 14, 15
V-Sit, 80

———————

W

Walking, 65
Wheelies, 68-70
    handstand, 82
Wheels, skateboard, 17-19, 20, 22, 38-43